Montezuma's®
CHOCOLATE
COOKBOOK

Simon and Helen Pattinson are ex-lawyers turned chocolate
makers who co-founded Montezuma's in 2000. They wanted
to bring innovation to a boring and staid British chocolate
market and their creative flavours, strong ethics and
delicious chocolate have made the brand a real success.

Montezuma's®

CHOCOLATE COOKBOOK

marvellous, messy, melt-in-the-mouth recipes

Simon & Helen Pattinson

photography by Clare Winfield

Kyle Books

We would like to dedicate this book to all the team at Montezuma's, who make coming to work each day fun and exciting; to our three girls, Poppy, Daisy and Isla, who don't tell many of their friends that Mum and Dad work in chocolate; and finally to our mums for their great home cooking.

First published in Great Britain in 2014 by
Kyle Books, an imprint of Kyle Cathie Ltd
192-8 Vauxhall Bridge Road
London SW1V 1DX
general.enquiries@kylebooks.com
www.kylebooks.com

Printer line 10 9 8 7 6 5 4 3 2 1

ISBN 978 0 85783 2 412

Editor: Tara O'Sullivan
Copy Editor: Emma Clegg
Designer: Carl Hodson
Photographer: Clare Winfield
Food Stylist: Rachel Wood
Prop Stylist: Iris Bromet
Production: Nic Jones and Gemma John

A Cataloguing in Publication record for this title is available from the British Library.

Colour reproduction by ALTA London
Printed and bound in China by C&C Offset Printing Co., Ltd.

This book is printed on paper from a sustainable source.

CONTENTS

introduction

As those bright sparks among you will have realised, our company name is an Anglicised form of the Aztec Emperor Motecuhzoma Xocoyotzin (Motecuhzoma II).

Nevertheless, for those who missed that history lesson at school, or possibly are still waiting for it, we have scrambled together a brief background to Monty and his love of chocolate.

In a nutshell, Monty was boss of the Aztecs and loved chocolate, the Spanish arrived to loot their riches, Monty got the idea that their leader, Hernán Cortés, was a returning god and so gave him chocolate.

In the beginning . . .

For some time, the history of cultivating and drinking chocolate, or to be more precise various mixtures made from cacao beans, has been thought to date back to about AD460 in what is now Guatemala.

However, discoveries in Belize show that an early Mayan civilisation were preparing cacao as early as 600BC. This discovery leaves 'hot chocolate' unchallenged as the world's oldest non-alcoholic beverage.

In about the early 1500s, the Aztec Empire covered central and southern Mexico, from the Pacific to the Atlantic. The unsuspecting Montezuma II was ruling his people from the capital of Tenochtitlan when the Spanish conquistadors arrived, led by Hernán Cortés.

Chocolatl and beyond

At this time, cocoa beans and cocoa pods were greatly valued by the Aztecs and are often depicted in the art from that period. Merchants traded them between the humid Mexican basin and the major Aztec cities, and it is thought that they were a form of currency.

The cocoa was also used in ceremonies, including ritual human sacrifice, where the heart of the victim was replaced with a cocoa pod: this didn't do much for their digestion or indeed the development of cocoa! Cocoa beans were consumed, mainly in the bitter and thick maize- and cocoa-based drink called chocolatl. It is somewhat unpalatable to modern tastes, despite some attempts to replicate the original recipes.

It was in this form that Montezuma drank up to 50 mugs a day in order to keep his harem smiling. The drink is also where the once common phrase 'Montezuma's revenge' derives from; the ingredients used acted as a mild laxative.

The increasingly unfortunate Aztecs wrongly assumed that the Spaniards were long-awaited returning gods and presented them with, among other things, Chocolatl. It was because of this formal and seemingly innocuous presentation that the Spanish took cocoa back to Spain, marking the beginning of chocolate consumption in Europe.

At least we can thank Imperialism for something useful, although the outcome for Emperor Montezuma II was not so positive. Poor old Monty was stoned to death by his own people, who gradually realised that Cortés was about as far from a saviour god as possible!

about montezuma's

We started Montezuma's, our great little chocolate business, in 2000 with only a kitchen sink-sized machine, huge enthusiasm, spades of naivety and, most importantly, a broad ideal to bring chocolate innovation to what we viewed as a boring and staid British chocolate market.

With the exception of that first machine, little has changed and the childish enthusiasm we shared exploring South America in 1999 largely wakes up with us every morning; although we now have three little girls who rise before dawn every day!

Being lawyers turned self-taught chocolate makers wasn't perhaps the expected path, but then again some may suggest lawyers aren't that great at very much! What we certainly didn't train for, or indeed expect in our wildest dreams, was that a business started on a shoestring would become arguably Britain's most innovative chocolate brand with a reputation far bigger than our actual footprint.

We still strive to bring exciting, high-quality and innovative chocolate to the everyday chocolate market and will never settle for the extremes of low-quality, vegetable fat-laden chocolate or excessively priced, boutique-styled chocolate that threatens to drive a wedge into what should be a general appreciation of a quality chocolate.

We hope to encourage everyone to appreciate good chocolate by making it accessible without the need to sign up for the nonsensical and somewhat pompous academies of good taste that have become the fashion among self-proclaimed 'foodies'. If you like, we subscribe to the school of thought that, could we legislate for good taste, good taste would cease to exist!

Our story

It seems incredible that the smell of chocolate was one of the things that made Helen and I want to abandon our careers in law. Having become totally disillusioned with London, law and all the trappings of an apparently glamorous career, we resigned, sold our London house, put all our possessions into storage and jumped on a plane for South America with everything in two rucksacks.

We cannot remember why South America attracted us, but I think it was probably the huge diversity of climates, cultures and landscapes. We were not disappointed and had a truly remarkable year wandering, climbing and generally rumbling around the vast continent. Although we had left the UK with a vague notion that we would be inspired to find a new direction, I don't think we ever imagined that this would really be the case and perhaps a return to law was on the cards on our return.

We both had a long-term love of chocolate, but a chocolate business was not something we had considered until we went to a little town in the middle of Argentina where a large German population ran several exciting chocolate shops. The chocolate smell throughout the town was all encompassing – we didn't realise at the time that this visit had planted a seed that was to develop over the next nine months.

This seed developed further when we reached Venezuela and accidentally ended up camping on a cocoa plantation. Fortunately, the plantation was a friendly mix of hectic farming and enthusiastic chilling, which provided plenty of opportunity to understand the fascinating complexity of cultivating quality cocoa. We witnessed cocoa being grown, harvested and processed into cocoa liquor, and soon realised that there was a lot more to chocolate than first meets the eye over the chocolate shop counter.

Having seen the delicate little cocoa tree and tasted many varieties, we could think of little else while hitchhiking around South America, and this business idea began to flourish into a sketch, and then a drawing, and eventually a full-blown plan.

Almost a year to the day that we returned from our travels, we opened our first store in Brighton, with more than 200 products ranging from organic chocolate lollies to huge boxes filled with chunky truffles. I only have to wander into one of our stores and listen to the customers' comments to know that we have made the right choice.

how chocolate is made

You would never begin to guess how complex this process is or how it ever developed to produce the chocolate we now love so much.

Growing the beans

Interestingly, about 80 per cent of the world cacao harvest is grown in 1- to 2-hectare estates: it's not big agribusiness, but small farm production.

The delicate and beautiful cocoa tree requires a consistent temperature and humidity level, together with protection from direct sunlight – this is often achieved by using shade from larger mother trees. These demands effectively limit the scope of cocoa growing to about 20 degrees either side of the equator.

Trees will produce fruit in about 4 years but can take 10 years to offer the very best mature fruit, although at no stage is there any indication that, after many steps, this fruit will produce something as wonderful as chocolate.

Preparing the beans

Once the pods are opened and the beans removed, they must be fermented. This varies from country to country, but on smaller plantations the beans are often fermented under banana leaves so that the cocoa can develop flavour. Once they are fermented and dried in the sun, they are cleaned, ready to be roasted.

Once roasted, the beans must be shelled or winnowed to reveal the nib from which the chocolate is made. The roasted nibs are now ready to be ground into a paste that will eventually become chocolate.

The first stage of grinding is to produce cocoa liquor from the nibs. This thick paste is somewhat misleadingly named as it isn't a liquid and more akin in viscosity to peanut butter. All designed to add to the mystery and confuse the unwary!

With a fat content of more than 50 per cent, at room temperature the solid cocoa butter suspends the other cocoa particles, which is more interesting when we begin to work with chocolate and attempt melting and tempering.

Effectively the final stage is to knead and mix the chocolate liquor and cocoa butter with other ingredients to make chocolate of various types. For milk chocolate, sugar and powdered milk are added, for dark chocolate no milk is needed but sugar is, while for white chocolate, cocoa butter without the other cocoa elements is added to milk and sugar. Often vanilla is added to all types of chocolate to help with the end notes in the flavour profile.

This 'grinding, refining and mixing' is achieved through a couple of processes that can take from several hours to many days depending on the depth of flavour and also on the age of the machinery.

The most well-known of these processes and most talked about is a stirring and milling process that removes moisture and acidity from the chocolate, which also increases the smoothness by reducing the particle size further.

At the end of this, one has to wonder how chocolate ever became developed and how the evolution of putting cocoa through such a complex process was invented!

cooking with chocolate

Patience

For me, every day with chocolate is different and every day brings a new focus. The more we try to control it, the more it throws us interesting challenges inviting creative solutions. For all this, however, chocolate rewards the patient and careful chocolatier with flavour and balance that blends strength and subtlety. All this while retaining a delightful delicacy that carries and complements flavours across the full spectrum of recipes and ingredients.

Despite this glorious potential, chocolate has a reputation for being a tricky ingredient among the massed ranks of professional chefs. This is especially so when being used for final coatings when a glossy and perfect finish is demanded.

In many ways this reputation is justified, however the techniques proposed in various books over the years vary from the downright ridiculous to the overly complex and entirely unjustified. This is almost always because any working method for chocolate must accept the essential nature of using chocolate in the kitchen: variability (see below).

When reflecting on these recipes, the focus is not on classic delights found in chocolate shops the world over, that is surely for another book, but more on recipes and methods that contain all the required techniques. This chapter is therefore little more than some words of caution and advice on the most basic but most critical element of working with chocolate.

More patience

Fundamentally, it is not possible to adequately control the variables of heating and cooling temperature, humidity, air flow and a number of other issues. Chocolate manufacturers spend significant efforts regulating these in order to achieve effective and constant quality. We must accept this by using methods that are simple and therefore not always foolproof!

The most basic of these techniques is the effective melting of chocolate so it becomes liquid without burning. If that melted chocolate is to then be used as an effective 'top coat' then appearance will be important and the chocolate will need to be cooled and set hard so it remains stable.

If simply left to cool without manipulation, chocolate can set into several slightly different chemical structures, only one of which is desirable for the aesthetically sensitive chef. Well-tempered chocolate not only looks better, but it is better to work and tastes better due to the refined melting pattern in the mouth.

Getting chocolate to set to the correct form is generally known as tempering and is the stuff of myth and complexity, and is frankly seen as the black art of the chocolatier. Given that the home environment does not lend itself to precise control, tempering needs to be accepted as at best slightly hit and miss and given the simplicity it deserves. I have used two very similar methods in the recipes and both work around 80 per cent of the time at home. However, the method detailed in the next section is marginally easier and marginally more reliable. Feel free to swap the methods if you find one easier (or less messy)!

3 golden rules for melting chocolate

①

Always melt chocolate in a bain-marie or heatproof bowl over water that boiled 5 minutes earlier and is now off the heat. Stir until smooth. Don't be tempted to rush this.

③ You can use a microwave by melting at 500w for 1 minute, stirring well, and then repeating the process with 30 second bursts 'and stirs' until smooth. Do not rush this process either.

② Do not add water to the chocolate to assist in any way as often suggested.

Tempering

There are many methods to achieve tempered chocolate, however most require very precise control of the variables that can affect the process. Almost all methods will give you temperatures to work to, normally with only a few degrees of tolerance. Given that chocolate heats and cools quickly and home thermometers are only accurate to about 3 degrees, this is extremely difficult to achieve and is often more to do with luck than skill. My method is also not foolproof, but it will be easy to repeat and won't make your kitchen look like piece of chocolate installation art!

This is a method to temper a total of 600g of chocolate in button-size pieces.

✶ Melt 400g of the chocolate in a bain-marie or heatproof bowl over water that boiled 5 minutes earlier and is now off the heat and cooling (this avoids burning the chocolate but also ensures the chocolate has been fully melted and de-tempered). Stir occasionally until smooth.

✶ Remove from the bain-marie and allow to sit for 5 minutes at room temperature (assuming your kitchen is about 20 degrees).

✶ Add the final 200g chocolate and stir with a spatula for a few minutes until smooth and melted.

✶ The chocolate should have come down to body temperature, which you can test by dabbing a small amount on your lip. If you feel neither hot nor cold, it is about right and tempered.

1

Sweet Treats

For me, nothing quite lives up to chocolate plus chocolate! Just calling it 'Double Chocolate' somehow fails to do justice to the simple concept of making chocolate sweets. We can mould it, flavour it, mix it and combine it to make beautifully subtle treats or bold and challenging flavours. Take these ideas as your entry into the expansive world of being a home chocolatier and get messy in the kitchen.

classic rocher

prep 30 minutes ✷ makes lots!

Also called a rock or cluster, this style of chocolate is a mainstay of many chocolatier ranges and a good, basic recipe and technique to learn. Oh yes, and they are always a firm favourite in our house – and so much better than many ready-to-buy alternatives.

100g granulated sugar
125g almonds, slivered
125g hazelnuts, chopped
300g dark chocolate, roughly
  chopped
40g white chocolate, grated

special equipment

bain-marie or heatproof bowl
petit-four cases

Preheat the oven to 150°C/gas mark 2. Line a baking tray with parchment paper.

Boil the sugar and 60ml water in a heavy-based pan over a medium heat. Boil rapidly for 5 minutes. Remove from the heat and stir in the nuts.

Spread the nut mixture on the prepared baking tray and roast until golden. This will take about 20 minutes, but watch the browning process carefully, as the nuts suddenly turn from gentle brown to burnt black. Cool the nuts on the baking tray.

Meanwhile, melt the dark chocolate in a bain-marie or a heatproof bowl over a pan of water that boiled 5 minutes earlier and is now off the heat and cooling. Stir occasionally until smooth.

Place the cooled nuts in a bowl and pour the chocolate in, stirring all the time, until the nuts are well coated.

Divide the mixture into petit-four cases, sprinkle with the grated white chocolate and leave the rochers to set at room temperature. These will keep for up to 3 months in the fridge in an airtight container.

TIP
If you make lots of these, store them in the fridge in an airtight container – and strictly ration!

clusters

prep 20 minutes ★ makes lots!

This is cooking with chocolate at its most simple, but the process is also lots of fun and can be enjoyed by all the family. This is the recipe that originally inspired my interest, not just in cooking, but in cooking with chocolate. As always, use a huge mixing bowl so the children have the opportunity to sample the contents throughout the process!

150g milk chocolate (you can try different mixes of chocolate)
75g crisped rice cereal
75g raisins and roasted nuts, roughly chopped (optional)

50g white chocolate

special equipment

bain-marie or heatproof bowl

Melt the chocolate in a bain-marie or a heatproof bowl over a pan of water that boiled 5 minutes earlier and is now off the heat and cooling. Stir occasionally until smooth.

You can now temper the chocolate, if you wish, which will make the cluster shiny and more professional looking. However, that adds another level of complexity, especially if you are cooking with children, so you might want to leave this for another time. (See page 12 for more about tempering chocolate.)

Combine the crisped rice into a large mixing bowl with any other dry ingredients. The raisins and roasted nuts are optional – you could also try using other ingredients of your choice, of a similar size to the crisped rice cereal.

Pour the melted chocolate over the ingredients and gently combine them. It is best to use as little chocolate as possible to cover all the ingredients, as otherwise the clusters become very hard to bite when set.

Spoon the mixture into little heaps on parchment paper. Leave to set at room temperature.

Meanwhile, melt a little white chocolate using the chocolate melting method above and drizzle this over the cakes for decoration. The clusters will keep for about 3 months in the fridge in an airtight container.

variations

Create layered clusters by making white ones first, then milk and then dark.

orangettes

prep 20 minutes, plus 24 hours drying ✳ makes lots!

This is a classic chocolatier technique that gives colourful and striking results. Everything depends on the quality of the chocolate, because all varieties of candied orange strips tend to taste similar. The key is to ensure the candied strips are as dry as possible and not overly sticky, and to make a good attempt at tempering the chocolate so it sets with a nice shine.

200g candied orange peel
  strips
icing sugar
350g dark chocolate, roughly
  chopped
5g ground cardamom

special equipment

bain-marie or heatproof bowl
small tongs or thin skewer

Dry the orange peel on a wire rack for 24 hours at room temperature. Then rub the peel in a little icing sugar to help remove more of the stickiness.

To temper the chocolate, melt the roughly chopped chocolate in a bain-marie or a heatproof bowl over a pan of water that boiled 5 minutes earlier and is now off the heat and cooling. Stir occasionally until smooth. Add the cardamom, if using.

Once melted, pour two thirds of the chocolate onto a cold, clean kitchen work surface (marble is ideal) and move/spread the chocolate with a spatula until it cools to body temperature (simply test this by putting a spot of chocolate on your lip – it needs to feel neither hot nor cold).

Transfer the cooled chocolate back to the still warm chocolate in the pan and combine them gently for about 1 minute.

Dip the strips of candied orange peel, one by one, into the chocolate. Either half dip them by hand or totally dip them using small tongs or a thin skewer. Put them on parchment paper and leave to set at room temperature. These will keep for about 3 months in the fridge in an airtight container.

This is a method of making a milk chocolate truffle with a smooth shell that doesn't need to be disguised by chocolate shavings. However, you can still use cocoa powder and icing sugar to decorate the outside should the shell chocolate fail you in some way. This simple method of making ganache allows you to play with variations in flavour, although the Classic Milk Truffle, which we call the 'milking maid', is hard to beat as long as the quality of the chocolate is excellent.

On that rather serious note, avoid chocolate with any vegetable fat in the ingredients list, and aim to use milk chocolate with a minimum of 40 per cent and up to 50 per cent cocoa solids. This creates a nice halfway house between dark and milk chocolate, but definitely remains on the dark side of chocolate making!

classic milk truffles

prep 35 minutes, plus 15 minutes chilling ∗ makes about 20 truffles

for the ganache

200ml double cream, or UHT
   cream
300g milk chocolate, roughly
   chopped

for the shell

400g milk chocolate, roughly
   chopped

200g milk chocolate, chopped
   to button size
unsweetened cocoa powder
   and icing sugar, for
   sprinkling (optional)

special equipment

bain-marie or heatproof bowl

To make the ganache, heat the cream in a pan until it just boils. Pour it over the roughly chopped chocolate and gently blend the mixture until smooth and glossy. The more you whisk the ganache, the stiffer it will become. Chill the ganache in the fridge for about 15–30 minutes so you can roll it by hand.

Remove your now-firm ganache from the fridge and use a teaspoon to scoop out a small amount at a time for hand-rolling into balls. Keep your hands cool, and do this quickly so the ganache doesn't soften too much in your hands. Set aside.

To make the shell, melt the roughly chopped chocolate in a bain-marie or a heatproof bowl over a pan of water that boiled 5 minutes earlier and is now off the heat and cooling. Stir occasionally until smooth.

Remove the chocolate from the bain-marie or bowl, and leave for 5 minutes at room temperature. Now add the button-size chocolate pieces and stir with a spatula for a few minutes until they are smooth and melted.

The chocolate should now have reached body temperature. Test this by putting a spot of chocolate on your lip – it needs to feel neither hot nor cold. Now it is ready for coating the ganache balls.

Use a fork or skewer to dip the ganache balls into the shell chocolate, one at a time. Gently wipe the excess chocolate on the edge of the bowl before placing them on some greaseproof paper and leave them to set at room temperature (or chill for 15 minutes in the fridge). If they come out shiny, allow them to warm to room temperature before serving. If they are dull, revert to plan B and sprinkle them with a 50:50 mix of cocoa powder and icing sugar.

These will keep for about 2 weeks in the fridge in an airtight container.

dark chocolate and vanilla truffles

prep 50 minutes, plus 45 minutes chilling ∗ makes about 20 truffles

for the ganache

125ml fresh double cream
2 whole vanilla pods
250g dark chocolate, finely
  chopped

for the shell

200g dark chocolate, roughly
  chopped

200g dark chocolate, grated
50g unsweetened cocoa
  powder (optional)

special equipment
bain-marie or a heatproof
  bowl

Place the cream in a heavy-based pan and bring to a simmer. Meanwhile, run a very sharp knife along the vanilla pods to open one side, add them to the cream and continue to simmer for about 5 minutes.

Take the pan off the heat and remove the pods. Using your thumbnail, gently push out the seeds from the pods into the cream. Cover the cream and vanilla mix with a cloth for a further 5 minutes.

Put the finely chopped chocolate in a bowl, pour over the still hot cream and stir until fully blended. This is your beautiful vanilla ganache. Put it in the fridge to chill.

The next stage is to prepare the shell. The tempering process takes 10 minutes; time it so the ganache has had 30 minutes in the fridge by the time the tempering is complete.

Melt the roughly chopped chocolate in a bain-marie or a heatproof bowl over a pan of water that boiled 5 minutes earlier and is now off the heat and cooling. Stir occasionally until smooth.

Once melted, pour two thirds of the chocolate onto a cold kitchen work surface (marble is ideal) and move/spread the chocolate with a spatula until it cools to body temperature (test this by putting a spot of chocolate on your lip – it needs to feel neither hot nor cold). Return the cooled chocolate to the still warm chocolate in the pan and mix gently for about 1 minute. This is now ready for dipping your ganache.

Remove your now-firm ganache from the fridge and use a teaspoon to scoop out a small amount for hand-rolling into balls. Do this quickly so it doesn't soften too much in your hands.

Once you have made all your balls, use a fork to dip them into the shell chocolate and then roll them in your chocolate gratings, or leave them to harden at room temperature and roll in cocoa powder

Place the balls on some greaseproof paper and leave them to set at room temperature, or chill for 15 minutes in the fridge.

The good old chocolate truffle can be seen as a 'black art' in the world of chocolate, using hidden ingredients, mysterious methods and traditions handed down from generation to generation. Fear not, this is a simple but delicious recipe for a dark chocolate and vanilla fresh cream truffle. Use dark chocolate with a full, rounded flavour and one that is not overly bitter. As an impartial observer, I would suggest any Montezuma's dark chocolate! We have shown a slightly different method of tempering to that for the Classic Milk Truffles (see page 23).

variations

There is a never-ending list of variations, but the broad choices are either to omit the vanilla pod, or leave it in and supplement it with other flavours.

Ground powders are easiest to work with. Start with something such as ginger powder and move on to raiding those little jars of spice at the back of the cupboard that never get used for anything; then work up to more unusual combinations such as Indian spices.

Another way to add flavour is to add food-grade essential oils. Only ever add one drop at a time and keep tasting as you go along – the warm ganache will generally taste twice as strong when hard and at room temperature.

double chocolate meringues

prep 30 minutes, plus 1 hour cooking ✷ makes 20–30

Decorated chocolate meringues make a great little dessert, or they can be used to accompany something grander, if required. We generally find they are set out on the table ready to party with another pudding, but when we return they have magically disappeared without a trace or a sound.

2 large egg whites
$\frac{1}{8}$ teaspoon salt
150g caster sugar
50g unsweetened cocoa
  powder
$\frac{1}{2}$ teaspoon almond extract
50g milk chocolate
30g icing sugar

special equipment

food-processor or blender
piping bag with a small- to
  medium-star tip

Preheat the oven to 130°C/gas mark 1 and line two baking trays with parchment paper.

Beat the egg whites with the salt until frothy. Using a food-processor or blender at high speed, gradually add the sugar, beating until stiff peaks start to form. Now fold in the cocoa powder and almond extract.

Using a piping bag with a small- to medium-star tip, pipe generous rosettes of the mixture onto the baking trays.

Bake the rosettes for about 50 minutes, until they are crisp and dry to the touch. Switch the oven off, but leave the meringues inside until they are completely dry. Put the meringues on a wire rack and leave them to cool to room temperature.

Melt the chocolate in a heatproof bowl over a pan of water that boiled 5 minutes earlier and is now off the heat and cooling. Stir occasionally until smooth.

Working in batches of 5 meringues at a time, use a teaspoon to drizzle chocolate over the meringues, before sieving icing sugar over the chocolate. Gently tap off the excess icing sugar. Serve as they are, or as an accompaniment to a dessert.

Everyone likes a good lollipop but sometimes, just sometimes, we like to experience that childhood memory within the realms of grown-up food. This is our very grown-up take on the chocolate lolly; it makes a stunning pudding and offers the chance for lots of variation. It is based on two chocolate discs sandwiching a chocolate ganache with a lollipop stick.

variations

Food-grade essential oils add delicate and unusual flavours, but must be used in very small doses, one drop at a time. Try orange, bergamot, mint or rose alone, or in combination.

lovely lollies

prep 1 hour, plus 1 hour cooling ∗ serves 4

for the chocolate discs

600g dark or milk chocolate, roughly chopped

for the chocolate ganache

135ml whipping or
UHT cream
230g dark or milk chocolate
(or a mixture), roughly
chopped

65g unsalted butter, softened
single drops of essential oils
(optional; see Variations)

special equipment

bain-marie or heatproof bowl
piping bag (if you have one)
lollipop sticks

Make the outside discs by melting 400g of the chocolate in a bain-marie or heatproof bowl over a pan of water that boiled 5 minutes earlier and is now off the heat and cooling. Stir occasionally, until smooth, before adding the remaining 200g chocolate. Continue stirring until smooth. The chocolate should have come down to body temperature. Test this by putting a spot of chocolate on your lip – it needs to feel neither hot nor cold.

Line a baking tray with greaseproof paper. Using either a piping bag or a spoon, drop 8 even-sized 'dollops' of the melted chocolate, spacing them roughly 5cm apart on the lined baking tray. Remember you need two dollops for each lollipop. Pick up the tray and give it a firm tap so the chocolate spreads out to form circles roughly 7cm across.

Set the tray aside and leave it to cool at room temperature (or if you are in a hurry, refrigerate the tray for 10 minutes). The chocolate should be very stable and retain a nice shine when set.

Now make the ganache. Pour the cream into a saucepan and bring it to simmering point. Remove from the heat and leave it to cool for a minute or two.

Put the 230g chopped chocolate in a bowl and pour over the still-warm cream. Stir until smooth before adding the softened butter. At this point, if you would like to, add any essential oils. Leave the ganache to cool for 1 hour in the fridge.

Now for the fun part – the assembly! Use a quarter of the ganache as a glue to sandwich two of the discs together, with a lollipop stick in the middle. Squash the discs gently so the ganache spreads out. Repeat with the remaining discs and ganache. These will keep for a few days in an airtight container in the fridge (the top shelf is best).

zesty orange squares

prep 1 hour, plus 2 hours chilling ✳ makes about 20

for the base

140g plain flour
2 tablespoons unsweetened
  cocoa powder
225g unsalted butter, melted
75g granulated sugar
55g icing sugar

for the orange layer

finely grated zest of 1 orange
100ml freshly squeezed orange
  juice or 2 drops of orange
  essential oil

45g cornflour
1 tablespoon unsalted butter,
  melted
100g smooth-style orange
  marmalade, without bits

for the topping

3½ tablespoons cream
2 teaspoons golden syrup
100g dark chocolate, grated

special equipment

20cm baking tin

To make the base, preheat the oven to 180°C/gas mark 4. Grease a 20cm baking tin and line it with parchment paper, leaving an overhang to make it easier to remove later.

Mix the flour and the cocoa in a bowl. Beat the butter, sugar and icing sugar in another bowl, until creamy. Lastly, gently beat in the flour and cocoa.

Firmly press the mixture into the base of the baking tin to create a smooth and even base layer. Prick the mixture all over with a fork and bake for 25–30 minutes, until firm to the touch. Leave to cool – this takes about 25 minutes.

To make the orange layer, mix the orange zest and juice (or oil) with 125ml water and the cornflour in a pan over a medium heat. Bring to a boil, stirring constantly, and keep stirring until thickened. Once it has thickened, remove from the heat and stir in the butter and marmalade.

Pour the orange mixture over the base and bake for 5 minutes. Cool completely and then chill for 1 hour.

To make the topping, bring the cream and golden syrup to the boil in a small pan. Remove from the heat and stir in the grated chocolate until it is melted and smooth.

Spread the chocolate over the middle to create your topping. Chill in the fridge for 1.5 hours, before carefully removing from the tin. Peel off the parchment paper and cut into squares.

These orange squares take me back to my mum's cooking and the peppermint version of this recipe she used to make. They came out looking just like these, except the green food colouring was so powerful the squares actually glowed in the dark while we jumped around like hyper-charged kids. There is possibly a link there, I now feel! We have gone for orange in this recipe, but feel free to try anything.

variations

You can make the filling any flavour you like, although I tend to use orange, mint or lemon.

kirsch cherries

prep 2 months ✳ makes 50

This recipe is a long-term process – for best results it needs two months. The best way to enjoy cherries in chocolate is to ensure they are very, very, very boozy and succulent, and that means giving them plenty of time to get drunk on the kirsch. The results won't give you a hangover (unless you eat the whole lot), but they will certainly make you happy!

50 fresh cherries, stoned with
   stalks, washed and dried
130g golden caster sugar
2 vanilla pods
500ml kirsch
icing sugar, for dusting
300g white fondant

400g dark chocolate, roughly
   chopped

special equipment

1500ml preserving jar
bain-marie or heatproof bowl

Put the cherries in the preserving jar, adding a few at a time and sprinkling with sugar between each addition. Continue to the top of the jar, packing them in quite tightly. Split open the vanilla pods and push them in among the cherries, then fill the jar completely with kirsch. Leave to drown for two months in a cool place.

When ready, drain off the alcohol (keep it for drinking, as it is very nice indeed!). Dry all the cherries, ensuring you don't damage the stalks. Dust the cherries with icing sugar to complete this drying stage.

Melt the fondant in a heavy pan over a low heat until it is a hot and white liquid (if it goes clear, it is too hot and needs to cool a little). Then dip your cherries into the fondant, one at a time, holding the stalk. Leave to cool on a baking tray lined with greaseproof paper.

Melt the roughly chopped chocolate in a bain-marie or a heatproof bowl over a pan of water that boiled 5 minutes earlier and is now off the heat and cooling. Stir occasionally until smooth.

Once melted, pour two thirds of the chocolate onto a clean, cold kitchen work surface and spread the chocolate with a spatula until it cools to body temperature (test this by putting a spot of chocolate on your lip – it needs to feel neither hot nor cold). Mix this cooled chocolate back into the still-warm chocolate and mix gently for about 1 minute. The tempered chocolate is now ready.

Holding the stalks, dip each cherry into the chocolate, ensuring a small part of the stalk is also coated, therefore sealing the cherry.

Leave the cherries to set at room temperature, before transferring to an airtight container for another two week wait. This is painful and will test your resolve, but the sugar will turn to alcohol and they are certainly worth the wait!

peppermint creams

prep 1 hour ∗ makes approx. 500g

Homemade peppermint creams are far superior to almost any mass-produced variety, with a few notable exceptions. I have applied the same ideas here that we use at Montezuma's to make our famous Dainty Dollops. Most notably, the peppermint oil is far superior to, and cleaner tasting than, any flavouring I have ever found. Short of infusing fresh mint, this will give the best result.

375g granulated sugar
2–8 drops peppermint oil
300g dark chocolate

special equipment

sugar thermometer
bain-marie or heatproof bowl

Create the centre fondant by putting the sugar with 125ml water in a pan over a moderate heat, stirring until the sugar has dissolved. Then, using a soft spatula or hard pastry brush dipped in cold water, give the sides of the pan a clean to ensure the last remaining grains of sugar are dissolved.

Bring the syrup to the boil until it reaches 115°C on the sugar thermometer. Remove from the heat and add the peppermint oil.

To set the centre of the syrup, pour it onto a cold and damp kitchen work surface and move the syrup around with a spatula. Be patient and work it for about 10 minutes, until it stiffens. If the mixture is stubbornly soft, you may have to leave it for a little longer, but it will stiffen.

Line a baking tray with parchment paper. To create the shape required, drop teaspoonfuls of the fondant onto the lined baking tray. Give the tray a firm tap on the work surface to make it flatten out into discs. Set aside until cold.

Melt the chocolate in a bain-marie or a heatproof bowl over water that boiled 5 minutes earlier and is now off the heat and cooling. Stir occasionally until smooth.

Once melted, temper the chocolate by pouring two thirds of it onto a clean, cold kitchen work surface (marble is ideal) and spreading the chocolate with a spatula until it cools to body temperature (test this by putting a spot on your lip – it needs to feel neither hot nor cold).

Mix the cooled chocolate back to the still warm chocolate in the pan and mix gently for about 1 minute.

Using a thin fork, dip your fondant centres into the chocolate, wiping off the excess chocolate on the side of the bowl. Leave the peppermint creams to set at room temperature. They will keep for about 2 months in the fridge in an airtight container.

white chocolate granola

prep 20 minutes, plus 45 minutes cooking and
90 minutes cooling * makes 15–25

With only three measurements to remember, this makes for a very easy and family-friendly recipe.

250g white chocolate
50g butter, plus extra for
 greasing
100g honey
100g almonds or hazelnuts,
 coarsely chopped
100g macadamia nuts, coarsely
 chopped
100g desiccated coconut
100g dried apricots, coarsely
 chopped

100g raisins or sultanas
50g plain flour, plus extra for
 dusting

special equipment

bain-marie or heatproof bowl
10 x 25cm baking tray

Preheat the oven to 180°C/gas mark 4. Butter and flour a 10 x 25cm baking tray and line it with parchment paper.

Melt the chocolate and butter together in a heatproof bowl or bain-marie over a pan of water that boiled 5 minutes earlier and is now off the heat and cooling. You have to be especially careful not to burn white chocolate and this process will help to avoid this. Stir occasionally until smooth.

Gently heat the honey in a small pan until it becomes runny.

Mix the almonds or hazelnuts, macadamias, coconut, apricots, raisins or sultanas and flour in a large bowl. Add the chocolate mixture and the honey. Stir well. Spoon the mixture into the prepared tin and bake for approximately 40–45 minutes, until golden.

Cool in the pan on a wire rack for 90 minutes before cutting.

variations

Try varying the dried fruits or replacing the white chocolate with milk or dark chocolate for a different flavour.

chocolate hens' eggs

prep 1 hour and 15 minutes, plus 45 minutes chilling ∗ makes 12 eggs

This is a fantastic way to get everyone involved in making Easter eggs, and these can be presented as real eggs hiding a sweet surprise. It is a novel and fun method, but it can get very messy, depending on how young the cooks are and how hard they shake the eggs. You have been warned, so stand well clear!

12 small eggs
600g dark chocolate
350ml double cream
170g hazelnut praline

special equipment

sewing needle
piping bag
eggbox or basket, for display

Preheat the oven to 150°C/gas mark 2. Use a needle to pierce a small hole in the end of each egg. Open the hole up to about 1cm using the sharp end of a knife.

Now gently shake the raw egg out. Using an oven glove to hold the egg and protect your hand, carefully pour boiling water into the shell and wash the inside several times. Dry the shells in the low oven for 20 minutes.

Melt the chocolate in a bain-marie or a heatproof bowl over a pan of water that boiled 5 minutes earlier and is now off the heat and cooling. Stir occasionally until smooth.

Pour the cream into a saucepan. Bring to the boil, remove from heat and stir in the chocolate. Stir in the praline.

Pipe the mixture into the eggshells until full. Clean the outsides and chill for at least 45 minutes. Present the finished eggs in an egg box or basket.

variations

Crack the shells of the eggs and peel them off for added fun. You could also try making these eggs with milk chocolate or white chocolate – or a mixture!

There is no chocolate quite like the chocolate on the shell of this annual treat at Easter. I still think it is one of life's great chocolate mysteries. Why do chocolate Easter eggs taste different from any other chocolate when they are made from the same ingredients?

I wanted to include this fun method for making a chocolate Easter egg because it doesn't involve heaps of expensive equipment and chocolate moulds (although these are increasingly available in good kitchen shops). I have tested the recipe many times, nearly always with my children 'assisting', and it works about 80 per cent of the time. If you get the first stage completed without a disaster, it will work 95 per cent of the time, but I can assure you that it is good fun 100 per cent of the time!

easter egg

prep 1 hour and 15 minutes ∗ makes 1 egg

600g chocolate, chopped into button-sized pieces (use any good-quality dark, white or milk chocolate, and it can be quite fun to create layers in different chocolates)

to decorate

melted chocolate to drizzle, sweets or nuts of your choice

special equipment

party balloon
pastry brush

Inflate the balloon to your desired Easter egg size and tie a knot. Don't get carried away the first time – stick to something about 15cm tall. Somewhere very close to the knot, stick a piece of tape about 2cm long, so that when you burst the balloon at the end it stays in one piece. We have occasionally found that some balloon latex can taint the chocolate, although most brands are fine. If you are concerned, test your chosen brand of balloons first with a small amount of chocolate – or you can carefully cover the balloon in clingfilm to act as a barrier, ensuring the film is also knotted at the same point.

You need to temper the chocolate so it is stable, easy to work with and sets with a pretty shine. Tempered chocolate also contracts slightly when set, making the moulding process easier. (See page 12 for more about tempering chocolate.)

Melt 400g of the chocolate in a bain-marie or a heatproof bowl over a pan of water that boiled 5 minutes earlier and is now off the heat and cooling. Stir occasionally until smooth.

Stir the chocolate, until smooth, for about 5 minutes, before adding the final 200g of button-sized chocolate pieces. Then stir with a spatula for a few minutes until smooth and fully melted. The chocolate should have come down to body temperature. Test this by putting a spot of chocolate on your lip – it needs to feel neither hot nor cold.

Take your balloon and, holding the knot, roll the chocolate in the tempered chocolate so all but the small area you are holding has a thin covering. It is best to start with a thin covering for the first layer.

When covered, leave the chocolate to set at room temperature, either laying the egg on its side, or, better still, sitting it knot-end down on top of a mug. Both ways leave a 'foot' of chocolate that will need gently trimming at the end. The chocolate should be largely set in 5–10 minutes.

One important tip here is that the chocolate can be kept at about 30°C and remain tempered for a short while, but you must not allow it to heat up. This is tricky, because if you boiled 2 litres of water that is now off the heat, depending on your pan, it will reach 30°C after about 15 minutes at a room temperature of about 20°C. Test the water against your lip in the same way, and when it is right, sit the chocolate over the water – this will help keep it tempered while you proceed with the next stages.

Continued overleaf

When almost set and not runny, repeat the process with a thicker layer. The chocolate will be thicker now, anyway, so this should be easy. Wait for the chocolate to set and repeat again. Three layers may be sufficient, but I would recommend one final layer with freshly tempered chocolate (repeat the second instruction, above). This could use a different coloured chocolate.

Using the tempered chocolate, make a disc slightly larger than the hole around the knot. You can make this disk flat, or for a more professional touch, make it on something with a similar curve to the top of the egg.

When the final layer is complete and set hard, gently trim off the 'foot' with a sharp knife. Using a pin, puncture the balloon where you applied the tape. It should go flat and be easily pulled out from the hollow egg.

The last stage is to attach your disk with some melted chocolate, before making cosmetic repairs to the shell using a brush and more tempered chocolate. This final stage is not necessary if you intend to decorate the egg. We always decorate the outside by sticking all manner of edible 'lovelies' on the outside, using melted chocolate as glue.

TIP.
When decorating the egg, stand it in a mug or something stable so you can turn it easily.

2

Cakes, Bakes & Pastries

In the UK everyone has gone baking mad, so we have to push forward chocolate as a versatile and delicious baking ingredient. Baking does not have to be an art only ever mastered by your mum – and it certainly isn't something that only people with 'bakers' hands' can secretly cosset. If you want some help deciding which to make first, go for Helen's Banana and Chocolate Loaf (page 46) and make sure you have friends to share it with.

TIP
Serve with fresh raspberries, which look fabulous and complement both the textures and flavours.

classic double chocolate roulade

prep 30 minutes, plus 20 minutes cooking
and 18 hours standing or chilling ∗ serves 8

There is not much to say about this classic roulade except that the white chocolate cream makes it just a little better than before! There are a host of variations you could try, using lots of different chocolate for the cream, including using chilli and lime for added interest.

120g dark chocolate
4 eggs, separated
110g golden caster sugar
icing sugar and unsweetened
  cocoa powder, for decoration

for the filling

200ml whipping cream
120g white chocolate, grated

special equipment

23 x 33cm Swiss roll tin
bain-marie or heatproof bowl

Preheat the oven to 180°C/gas mark 4. Line the tin with parchment paper.

Melt the chocolate in a bain-marie or heatproof bowl over a pan of water that has boiled 5 minutes earlier and is now off the heat. Once melted, set aside to cool.

Whisk the egg yolks and sugar in a bowl until they are pale and mousse-like. Fold in the cooling chocolate.

Whisk the egg whites in another bowl until stiff peaks start to form. Fold the whites into the chocolate mix. Pour this mixture into the tin and bake for about 15–20 minutes until firm. Remove from the oven, cover with a clean, damp tea-towel and leave to rest overnight.

Heat the cream for the filling in a pan until simmering (not boiling). Use a blender to combine the cream with the white chocolate until smooth. Pour the filling into a bowl and chill for 8 hours to thicken.

When ready to assemble the roulade, sift some icing sugar over a sheet of greaseproof paper that is larger than the roulade sponge. Turn out the roulade sponge onto the paper, taking care to remove the lining paper.

Whip the chocolate cream filling until soft peaks start to form, and spread this evenly over the roulade. Carefully roll the roulade up along the long side. Place on a serving dish, seam downwards, and chill for 2–3 hours until firm and ready to serve.

variations

The alcohol can be varied to create different flavours – try it with rum or Grand Marnier, for example. Orange juice works well for an alcohol-free version.

helen's banana and chocolate loaf

prep 30 minutes, plus 1 hour 15 minutes baking ✱ serves 15

This was the last recipe I worked on when drafting the book. I had scraps of paper everywhere from many years of collecting and refining ideas, but this is a gem from Helen, and is a favourite family treat when at home, out cycling or walking, or just about anywhere. Our larder isn't often without this chocolate loaf in some stage of consumption.

440g ripe bananas, peeled
  (weight without skins)
1 tablespoon lemon juice
225g dark chocolate, roughly
  chopped
300g self-raising flour
1 teaspoon baking powder
2 eggs, beaten

125g unsalted butter, melted,
  plus extra for greasing
125g caster sugar
banana chips, for decoration

special equipment

1kg loaf tin

Preheat the oven to 160°C/gas mark 3. Mash the bananas and the lemon juice together.

In a large bowl, mix together the mashed bananas, chopped chocolate, flour, baking powder, beaten eggs, melted butter and sugar.

Grease the loaf tin well, and line it with parchment paper to make it easier to get the loaf out in one piece. Spoon the mixture into the tin and decorate with banana chips.

Bake for 70–75 minutes until the loaf is well risen and the top has cracked. You know it is ready when you can insert a skewer and it comes out cleanly.

Cool the loaf in the tin for 10 minutes and then ease it out onto a wire rack. Cool completely before slicing.

double chocolate gâteau

prep 1 hour, plus 2 hours chilling ✴ serves 10

Helen first introduced me to her parents six weeks after we began dating. This was the same day we announced we wanted to get married in four months' time, the day we managed to set the barbecue on fire and also the day Helen's mum showed me her now famous double chocolate gateau. Best served at engagement barbecues.

250g unsalted butter, plus extra for greasing
250g golden caster sugar
4 eggs, beaten
185g self-raising flour
50g unsweetened cocoa powder

for the filling

200g white chocolate, chopped
210ml whipping cream

for the icing

300g dark chocolate, grated
100g unsalted butter
75ml double cream

for the decoration

100g dark or milk chocolate, grated

special equipment

20cm cake tin
food-processor or blender

Grease the cake tin and line with baking parchment. To make the filling, chop the white chocolate using a food-processor or blender in short bursts of a few seconds. Heat the cream in a pan until simmering, and then add the cream to the chocolate while the processor is running. When smooth, allow to cool in a bowl for 2–3 hours until firm. Before use, whisk the filling until firm peaks start to form.

Preheat the oven to 180°C/gas mark 4. Make the sponge by beating the butter and sugar in a bowl until light and fluffy, then beating in the eggs. In another bowl, sift the flour and the cocoa before folding them into the first mixture.

Spoon the mixture evenly into the tin and bake for about 40–55 minutes until an inserted skewer comes out cleanly. Allow to cool completely on a wire rack.

Meanwhile, make the icing. Melt the chocolate in a bain-marie or heatproof bowl over a pan of water that has boiled and is now off the heat and cooling. Add the butter and cream, stirring constantly as it cools to form a thick, spreadable mixture.

Using a bread knife, slice the sponge into three layers. Use the filling to sandwich all the layers together. Cover the top and sides with the icing and sprinkle the grated chocolate over the gâteau, to decorate.

black forest gâteau

prep 45 minutes, plus 35 minutes baking,
plus 2 hours chilling ∗ serves 12–16

Otherwise known as a black cherry torte, this was one of those 1970s dishes that lost favour within the pace of fast-moving food fashions. It never really lost favour with my mum, however, who had any number of variations that made it more appealing to children who never really understood the cherry and chocolate combination. How things have changed – and now the flavour combinations in a well-made classic black forest gateau are a match for any fancy recipe newcomer!

for the cake

butter, for greasing
8 eggs
190g caster sugar
1 teaspoon vanilla extract
210g dark chocolate
160g plain flour, sifted

for the filling and decoration

1kg fresh cherries (Morello are the best for this), stoned and washed

85g granulated sugar
120ml kirsch
1 litre double cream
1 tablespoon caster sugar
dark chocolate curls or grated dark chocolate
fresh cherries, stoned and washed

special equipment

2 x 23cm baking tins
bain-marie or heatproof bowl

Preheat the oven to 180°C/gas mark 4. Grease the baking tins and line with parchment paper.

Break the eggs into a large heatproof bowl and beat in the 190g caster sugar. Place the bowl over a pan of simmering water for about 8 minutes, until the mixture has doubled in volume and is thickening. Then beat in the vanilla extract.

Melt the chocolate and 120ml water (at room temperature) together, in a bain-marie or heatproof bowl over a pan of water that boiled 5 minutes earlier and is now off the heat and cooling. Stir occasionally until smooth.

Sift the flour over the egg mixture, folding a small amount in at a time before folding in the warm (but not hot) chocolate and water mixture.

Divide the mixture equally between the 2 lined tins and bake for approximately 30–40 minutes or until a skewer comes out cleanly from the centre of the cake. Once removed from the oven, leave to sit in the tins for a few minutes before turning the cakes on to wire racks to cool completely.

To make the filling, simmer the cherries, granulated sugar and 4 tablespoons of water in a pan until the cherries are soft – this will take about 5 minutes. Strain the mixture and keep the juices. Mix 70ml of the juice with 70ml of the kirsch and set aside in a separate cup.

Whip the cream to soft peaks before beating in the 2 tablespoons caster sugar. Fold in the remaining kirsch.

Once cooled, cut each cake horizontally into two equal layers. Put one layer on a flat plate and sprinkle with some of the kirsch and cherry mix from the set-aside cup, before covering it with some of the whipped cream (about 15–20 per cent of the total amount) and some cherries. Place the second cake layer on top, and again sprinkle with syrup and add cream and cherries.

Onwards and upwards, put a third cake layer on top, sprinkle with the remaining kirsch syrup and spread on yet more cream and cherries. Finish with the last cake layer and neatly coat the top and sides of the entire cake with the remaining cream.

Finish the cake by placing the curls or grated chocolate over the top and sides, and arranging the remaining cherries on top in a beautiful forest of red. Chill thoroughly in the fridge for a couple of hours until set firm.

panforte

prep 40 minutes, plus 40 minutes baking ∗ serves 8–16

Nutty, fruity, chocolatey and originally a traditional Italian recipe, this dish was apparently used to pay tax to the Catholic Church. Perhaps a new idea for tax collectors today! This keeps really well in an airtight box and is a great picnic food.

130g hazelnuts
50g brazil nuts
130g whole almonds, blanched
zest of 1 lemon, finely grated
130g candied fruits, roughly chopped (use cherry, orange or lemon)
130g dried dates, quartered
75g plain flour
2 tablespoons unsweetened cocoa powder
½ teaspoon cinnamon

½ teaspoon ground nutmeg
¼ teaspoon ground cardamom
250g honey
110g caster sugar
60g butter, plus extra for greasing
icing sugar, to dust

special equipment

blender or food-processor
22cm springform tin

Preheat the oven to 180°C/gas mark 4. Place the hazelnuts and brazil nuts on a baking tray and toast until golden but not burnt – this will take about 10 minutes, but watch them carefully. Use a blender or food-processor to roughly chop the toasted nuts and whole almonds before combining them in a large bowl with the zest, candied fruits, figs or dates, flour, cocoa and spices.

Reduce the oven temperature to 150°C/gas mark 2. Grease a 22cm springform tin and line it with parchment paper.

Very gently heat the honey, sugar and butter in a pan, stirring constantly until it reaches a soft ball stage. (You can test the temperature by dropping a small amount of the syrup into cold water. If it forms a soft and flexible ball that flattens when removed from the water, you have it perfectly heated.) Pour the mixture into the bowl with the nuts and other ingredients and stir to combine.

While the mixture is still warm, quickly spoon it into the buttered tin and bake for 35–40 minutes.

When you remove the panforte from the oven, it will appear uncooked, but it hardens and sets as it cools on a rack. Finish with a generous dusting of icing sugar.

torta di patate

prep 30 minutes, plus 1 hour cooking and
30 mins cooling ∗ serves 8

I admit that 'potato cake' doesn't sound very appetising, and that's partly
why we used the Italian name, hoping it would lure in the unsuspecting!
Presumably as you are reading this, you fall into one of three camps: you
were fooled by the title, you are intrigued by the idea, or you have had
torta di patate before and know how good it can be.

200g potatoes (such as
  Désirée), peeled
50ml whole milk
300g plain flour, plus extra for
  dusting
75g unsweetened cocoa
  powder
2½ teaspoons baking powder
¼ teaspoon salt
125g unsalted butter, plus
  extra for greasing
150g granulated sugar
3 large eggs
125ml milk

for the buttercream

75g unsalted butter
550g icing sugar
4 tablespoons whole milk
1½ teaspoons vanilla extract
2 drops lime essential oil

special equipment

25cm tube pan, or a
  circular cake pan with
  a small ramekin

Put the potatoes in a pan with just enough water to cover them. Bring to the boil,
cover with a lid and simmer for 20 minutes or until tender, and drain. Do not add
seasoning. Bring the 50ml milk to the boil in a separate pan and pour it over the
potatoes. Mash the potatoes until smooth, and leave to cool.

Preheat the oven to 180°C/gas mark 4. Grease and flour a 25cm tube pan (or
improvise by using a circular cake pan and putting a small ramekin in the centre
facing up the right way).

Mix the flour, cocoa, baking powder and salt in a bowl. Beat the butter and sugar
in another bowl, until creamy. Add the eggs, one at a time, beating until just
blended. Slowly and gradually beat the mashed potato into the mixture, followed
by all the dry ingredients, and finally the 125ml milk.

Empty the batter into the tube pan and bake for about 30–40 minutes, until a thin
skewer comes out cleanly. Leave the cake to cool for about 30 minutes in the pan
before turning out on to a wire rack.

Meanwhile, make the buttercream. Beat the butter in a bowl until fluffy. Gradually
add half of the icing sugar, beating well. Slowly beat in half of the milk and the
vanilla, followed by the remaining sugar and the lime oil. Add more milk if the
consistency isn't spreadable.

Coat the outside of the cake with the buttercream and serve.

chocolate-chip brioche

prep 30 minutes, plus 4 hours rising, plus 2 hours chilling, plus 10 minutes baking ✷ makes 12–16 mini brioches

It is a shame that brioche isn't a more regular visitor to our dinner table. The fact that I absolutely love the light and slightly puffy texture and sweet taste will come as no surprise – and nor will the fact that the addition of chocolate chips makes this a top recipe for a chocolate man such as myself. This was originally made to combine with our Hot Chocolate Soup recipe on page 129.

7g active dried yeast
100ml whole milk, warmed, plus 1 teaspoon
2 tablespoons caster sugar
½ teaspoon salt
500g plain flour, plus extra for dusting
340g butter, soft, plus melted butter for greasing

4 large eggs, lightly beaten, plus 1 yolk
65g dark chocolate, finely chopped

special equipment

16 small brioche moulds

Place the yeast, 100ml warm milk, sugar and salt in a small bowl. Stir gently and rest for 10 minutes.

Put the flour in a large bowl and pour in the yeast mixture before adding the butter. Beat the mixture slowly whilst gradually adding the 4 whole eggs. Knead the dough on a lightly floured board for about 5 minutes until soft and smooth.

Add the finely chopped chocolate to the dough, and continue kneading until well combined. Cover and leave in a warm place until it has doubled in volume, which will take between 1 and 2 hours. When doubled, flip out the dough onto a floured surface and knock back the dough (by giving it a couple of firm punches and another quick knead) to get rid of any unwanted air pockets that have formed. You may need to repeat this a few times. Then refrigerate for 2–3 hours.

Preheat the oven to 200°C/gas mark 6 and grease the small brioche moulds with melted butter. Weigh out 16 x 30g pieces of dough for the bases and 16 x 10g pieces for the tops. Roll each of these into a tight ball and put the larger balls in the bases of the moulds. Make a small dent in the top of each of the large balls and gently push a smaller ball into each until about a third of the smaller ball is buried. You can pinch the smaller ball a little so that it has a shape that fits neatly in the hole.

Lightly beat the egg yolk with the teaspoon of milk and use it to glaze the brioches. Cover them with a cloth in a warm place for about 30 minutes to double in volume. Brush with the glaze again and bake for about 10 minutes until golden.

variations

There are thousands of potential flavour additions, including some very delicate flavours using essential oils. Orange and rose geranium are fantastic, but use only a drop or two as the flavours are very strong and will taste slightly soapy if not used subtly.

brownies

prep 30 minutes, plus 30 minutes baking * makes 15–20

Everyone loves chocolate brownies, and everyone knows the difference between enjoying a delicate and moist baked delight and enduring a dried-out chunk of chocolate and flour. This recipe will (if the God of Baking isn't having a day off) result in a lovely, soft and chocolatey brownie that will be fabulously rich. You can bake them for a few more minutes if you prefer a slightly firmer brownie, or indeed change the proportion of dark to milk chocolate for a sweeter finish.

135g unsalted butter, plus
 extra for greasing
265g dark chocolate, chopped
4 large eggs
265g granulated sugar
80g light brown sugar
1½ teaspoons vanilla extract

160g plain flour
225g milk chocolate, chopped

special equipment

33 x 23cm baking tin
bain-marie or heatproof bowl
electric whisk (optional)

Preheat the oven to 180°C/gas mark 4. Grease the baking tin and line it with parchment paper, leaving lots of overhang to make removal easier at the end.

Melt the butter and dark chocolate in a bain-marie or heatproof bowl over a pan of barely simmering water that boiled 5 minutes earlier and is now off the heat and cooling. Stir occasionally until smooth. Remove from the pan when the chocolate is fully melted and mixed. Leave to cool.

Beat the eggs and both types of sugar in a bowl until thick and creamy. This is much easier with an electric whisk as it needs to be done at a high speed.

When creamy, beat in the cooled chocolate mixture, followed by the vanilla extract. Now add the flour and the milk chocolate.

Pour the mixture into the tin and bake until set in the middle – this will take anything from 20–30 minutes, depending on your oven. This is where most baking goes wrong, because you cannot rely entirely on the time given and you must check – for this mixture, I prefer to remove it from the oven when an inserted skewer comes out with a smear of mixture visible, so not entirely clean.

When ready, cool in the tin for 5 minutes before removing the brownies on the parchment paper to a wire rack for 30 minutes and then giving them 15 minutes in the fridge. When cool, remove the parchment paper and cut with a bread knife.

highland brownies

We have already delved into the world of chocolate brownies, but like so many things chocolatey, there are lots of variations and inspirations to pursue. This is my very favourite brownie, using not only whisky (Scottish Malt, no less), but also crowned with a frosting.

140g plain flour
½ teaspoon baking soda
generous pinch salt
80g unsalted butter, plus extra
  for greasing
140g granulated sugar
70ml whisky (we use the
  slightly smoky Bowmore
  Islay Single Malt)
200g dark chocolate, chopped
1 teaspoon vanilla extract
2 large eggs
150g hazelnuts, roughly
  chopped

for the frosting

225g dark chocolate, roughly
  chopped
225ml milk
225g unsalted butter
190g granulated sugar
1 teaspoon vanilla extract

special equipment

bain-marie or heatproof bowl
20cm square baking tin

First make the frosting. Melt the roughly chopped chocolate in a bain-marie or a heatproof bowl over a pan of water that boiled 5 minutes earlier and is now off the heat and cooling. Stir occasionally until smooth. Gradually beat in the milk and then simmer, stirring constantly, until thickened. Remove the chocolate from the heat and leave to cool to room temperature.

Beat the butter, sugar and vanilla in a bowl until creamy before gradually beating into the chocolate mixture.

To make the brownies, preheat the oven to 160°C/gas mark 3. Grease the baking tin and line with parchment paper.

Mix the flour, baking soda and salt in a bowl. Place the butter and sugar in a pan over a low heat and add 2 tablespoons water and the whisky, chocolate and vanilla. Keep stirring until smooth.

Add the eggs to the butter-and-sugar mixture, one at a time, beating all the time. Stir in the mixed dry ingredients and the hazelnuts. Spoon the batter into the prepared tin.

Bake for about 25 minutes until you can insert a skewer and it comes out slightly sticky and not clean. Cool completely in the tin before frosting the brownies ready for slicing and eating.

chocolate scones

prep 10 minutes, plus 15 minutes baking ✶ makes 12 scones

My mother-in-law tells me that a Devonshire Cream Tea is one of the great food pleasures in life. Now, while I am never one to quibble semantics – least of all with one of the Tea-Time Generation – I did challenge myself to make a scone that could increase that pleasure markedly. This chocolate scone was the result, and while I still haven't been able to test the results on those who really matter, I do think they improve an already wonderful combination when served with Devonshire clotted cream.

260g self-raising flour
100g unsalted butter, cubed,
    plus extra for greasing
2½ tablespoons caster sugar
70g dark chocolate, roughly
    chopped

220ml whole milk, plus extra
    for glazing
plain flour, for coating work
    surface
clotted cream, to serve

Preheat the oven to 220°C/gas mark 7 and grease a baking tray.

Rub the flour and butter in a bowl until the mixture begins to resemble breadcrumbs. Then stir in the sugar and chocolate. Gradually pour in the milk so the mixture forms a soft dough.

Flour your work surface and roll out the dough until it is about 2.5cm thick. This should make a rectangle about 15 x 20cm – cut this into 12 squares.

Spread out the squares on the baking tray, leaving plenty of room in-between each one as they will expand in all directions. Brush the squares with some milk and bake for 10–15 minutes until they are golden and quite a lot bigger.

Serve the scones slightly warm with clotted cream.

hazelnut and coffee biscotti

prep 30 minutes, plus 30 minutes baking * makes lots!

These are crunchy biscuits to our kids, but cut them in that special elongated way and we call them biscotti. The dough is easy to make, and they are even easier to eat, particularly with a quality espresso or even a glass of something sweet, such as a fine Pedro Ximénez sherry.

120g hazelnuts
280g plain flour
70g unsweetened cocoa
  powder
2 teaspoons baking soda
3 large eggs
175g caster sugar
½ teaspoon vanilla extract

6 tablespoons very (very)
  strong coffee
80g dark chocolate, chopped
butter, for greasing

special equipment

food-processor or blender

Preheat the oven to 160°C/gas mark 3.

Spread the hazelnuts on a baking tray and toast until lightly golden but not burnt. This will take about 5 minutes, but watch them like a hawk! Remove from the oven and, once cooled, rub them in a tea-towel to remove the skins.

Increase the oven temperature to 190°C/gas mark 5.

Mix the flour, cocoa and baking soda in one bowl and beat the eggs, sugar and vanilla in another, until creamy. Gradually beat the dry ingredients into the egg and sugar mixture.

Now gradually beat in the coffee, dark chocolate and hazelnuts to form a stiff dough.

Split the dough in half and form two 30cm logs. Place them on a greased baking tray about 10cm apart. Flatten them slightly so they take on the biscotti shape.

Bake for about 25–30 minutes until the logs are firm but not hard. Remove from the oven and allow to cool.

Once cool, cut the logs diagonally into 1cm slices. Place on a lined baking tray and bake at 160°C/gas mark 3 for 10 minutes. This is the final crisping phase.

Cool on a wire rack before serving.

marbled three-nut 'get-going' bars

prep 50 minutes, plus 25 minutes baking,
plus 1 hour chilling ∗ makes loads

120g unsalted, unroasted nuts
  (pecans, peanuts and cashew
  nuts)
50g dried apricots
50g sultanas
100g porridge oats
25g bran flakes, gently broken up
25g crisped rice cereal
1 teaspoon black treacle or
  molasses syrup
250ml condensed milk

for the topping

150g very dark chocolate,
  minimum 73 per cent cocoa
  solids
75g white chocolate

special equipment

baking tray measuring 5 x 20
  x 20cm
bain-marie or heatproof bowl

Preheat the oven to 180°C/gas mark 4. Roast your peanuts, pecan and cashew nuts on a baking tray for 5 minutes. When roasting these little beauties, keep an eye on them and ensure they are golden and not burnt! Leave to cool.

Take the cooled nuts and the apricots and chop them roughly so they are about the same size. Mix together with the sultanas, oats, bran flakes and crisped rice.

Next is the sticky bit that our three little girls love to help with. Line a 20 x 20cm baking tray with parchment paper. Gently heat the molasses and the condensed milk until warm and fully blended, and then add the fruit and nut mix. Put this mixture into the baking tray and press down reasonably firmly with a tablespoon.

Bake the base mixture for 20–25 minutes until it is golden and not burnt. Leave to cool.

Get the chocolate topping ready by melting the dark and white chocolate separately in a bain-marie or a heatproof bowl over a pan of water that boiled 5 minutes earlier and is now off the heat and cooling. Stir occasionally until smooth. This stops the chocolate burning.

Once the base mixture is cool, carefully turn over the tray and turn out the solid mix on to a board or cooling rack.

Pour the dark chocolate on top of the base mixture and then add the white chocolate. Spread the topping with a palette knife to give a generous marbled chocolate top. Chill in the fridge for 1 hour and then chop into suitable sized bars.

As a keen outdoor and sporty family, we are forever battling to find a great energy food that hits the spot and is easy to pack away; plainly it also has to have our daily chocolate hit! This recipe was designed around texture and flavour, largely dictated by my then five-year-old daughter who decided that learning to ride without stabilisers is as worthy of a treat as a family trek around the South Downs. Who am I to argue? By the way, these energy bars taste just as good luxuriating in front of the TV watching a Sunday afternoon Audrey Hepburn film.

chocolate and geranium madeleines

prep 30 minutes, plus 1 hour 30 minutes
chilling and cooking ★ makes 12–18

These are, in reality, little cakes, although the term 'madeleine' usually means they are baked in the traditional shell-like shape that makes them all too easy to scoff at quite a rate! The use of geranium with chocolate is a combination we have played with for many years in various creations, including a best-selling chocolate bar. In freshly baked cakes, these flavours take on a delicate, floral personality that is very appealing and unusual. These cakes should be light and fluffy.

80g plain flour, plus extra for dusting
1 teaspoon baking powder
40g unsweetened cocoa powder
3 large eggs
110g caster sugar
2 tablespoons golden syrup
1 teaspoon vanilla extract

1–2 drops rose geranium essential oil
120g unsalted butter, melted, plus extra for coating the tin

special equipment

madeleine tin (normally holds 12–18 cakes)

Gently sift the flour and baking powder and cocoa powder in a small bowl. In another, larger bowl, whisk together the eggs, sugar, syrup, vanilla extract and a few drops of essential oil, until pale and foamy. Then fold in the flour mix from the smaller bowl. Gently and slowly fold in the melted butter.

Cover the mixture with clingfilm, ensuring that it touches the top of the mixture to prevent air bubbles forming. Chill in the fridge for 1 hour.

Preheat the oven to 230°C/gas mark 8. Coat the madeleine tin in melted butter before setting the butter by placing the tin in the fridge for 30 minutes. When set, dust the tin with some flour.

Take the tin and mixture out of the fridge and fill each cavity until almost full.

Bake for 4 minutes, then reduce the oven temperature to 200°C/gas mark 6 and bake for a further 4 minutes. Remove from the oven and tap the madeleines out of the tin on to a wire rack to cool.

chocolate macaroons with lime buttercream

prep 1 hour, plus 24 hours 'resting' ∗ makes about 30

270g icing sugar, sifted
130g ground almonds
25g unsweetened cocoa
  powder
4 egg whites
pinch of salt

for the buttercream

75g unsalted butter

550g icing sugar
2–4 tablespoons whole milk
1½ teaspoons vanilla extract
2 drops lime essential oil

special equipment

blender or food-processor
piping bag with a size 10
  nozzle

Preheat the oven to 200°C/gas mark 6. Line a baking tray with parchment paper. Blend the icing sugar, almonds and cocoa in a blender or food-processor for about 1 minute.

Whisk the egg whites with the salt until stiff peaks start to form, and gently fold in the almond mixture.

Now the fun bit! Pipe the macaroon mix on to the lined baking tray. You should be able to pipe about 60 small macaroons measuring about 4cm in diameter.

If possible (without causing a heat hazard in your kitchen!), bake the macaroons for 6–10 minutes with the oven door slightly ajar so the steam doesn't build up in the oven. Cool on a wire rack.

Meanwhile, make the buttercream by beating the butter in a bowl until fluffy. Gradually add half of the icing sugar and beat the mixture well. Beat in 2 tablespoons of the milk with the vanilla, followed by the remaining icing sugar and the drops of lime oil. Add more milk if the consistency isn't quite spreadable.

Now make the macaroon sandwiches with a thin layer of buttercream as the glue. Put all the macaroons in an airtight container for 24 hours – over this time they will develop a chewy texture.

Macaroons are very fashionable currently, along with cupcakes and all things 'buttercreamed'. Having said that, there are good and bad macaroons. The best ones I ever tasted were from Patisserie Academie in Bruges – I think these get close to those masterpieces.

salted pecan and chocolate pie

prep 20 minutes, plus 45 minutes cooking ✻ serves 8

Despite the good people of Louisiana claiming pecan pie as their own (as well as some of my favourite banjo music in Swamp Blues), the history is not well known and variations exist just about everywhere, including in France, New Orleans and deepest West Sussex. This salted chocolate pecan pie is of our making, although we don't use corn syrup (so often found in US recipes), preferring the richer flavour of golden syrup. We have cheated here by using a packet of premade shortcrust pastry. The pie is quite tricky to cut, but well worth it.

320g premade shortcrust
  pastry sheet
plain flour, for dusting
50g unsalted butter
3 tablespoons unsweetened
  cocoa powder
225ml golden syrup
3 eggs

80g muscovado sugar
200g pecan nuts
pinch of sea salt
whipped cream or ice cream,
  to serve

special equipment

20cm flan tin

Preheat the oven to 190°C/gas mark 5.

Roll out the pastry on a lightly floured surface and line the flan tin with parchment paper. Make the filling by melting the butter in a heavy pan before adding the cocoa and syrup.

Beat the eggs and sugar together in a large bowl before adding to the syrup mixture, along with the pecans and salt. Stir until fully blended and pour into the pastry case.

Bake for about 40 minutes, or until the filling is set but not drying out too much. Leave the pie to cool slightly before serving with whipped cream or ice cream.

variations

Try adding a drop or two of rum – or replace the shortcrust pastry with chocolate pastry!

nut and chocolate strudel

prep 1 hour, including baking ✳ serves 6

We came across this at our friends' house last summer, although I had to work hard to get them to relinquish the family recipe. It is a delectable combination of crunchy filo pastry, nuts and, of course, dark chocolate. We have cheated (again, I hear you say!) and used premade filo pastry.

100g blanched almonds
100g shelled and unsalted
  pistachios
100g walnut pieces
75g unsalted butter
75g light muscovado sugar
75g dark chocolate, finely
  chopped
200g filo pastry
whipped cream, to serve

for the syrup

110g caster sugar
1 teaspoon lemon juice
2 tablespoons honey
1–2 drops orange essential oil

special equipment

food-processor or blender

Preheat the oven to 180°C/gas mark 4. Line a baking tray with parchment paper. Using a blender or food-processor, chop the nuts until coarse, and then stir them over a low heat in a frying pan until they begin to brown. Don't overcook.

Remove the nuts from the heat and stir in the butter and sugar. Once cool, mix in the chocolate.

Overlap the filo sheets to make one large sheet measuring approximately 90 x 65cm. Sprinkle the filling evenly over the pastry and carefully roll it up.

Turn the roll into a crescent and tuck both ends underneath. Bake on the lined baking tray for about 25 minutes until the strudel is golden brown. Remove and leave to cool in the tin.

Meanwhile, make the syrup by heating the sugar and 100ml water gently in a pan until dissolved, stirring constantly.

Bring to the boil, add the lemon juice and honey and simmer for 10 minutes until syrupy. Leave to cool for 5 minutes and add the orange oil drops, one at a time, to create a subtle taste.

Pour the hot syrup over the strudel, cut it into thick slices and serve with whipped cream.

chocolate and pistachio filo parcels

prep 10 minutes, plus 20 minutes baking, plus
10 minutes cooling ✳ makes 20

The taste of pistachio has always been slightly mysterious, full of Eastern promise but rarely delivering as an ingredient in recipes. These delicate little nuts always seem to fade from their original flavour unless they are balanced really carefully. To be honest, my residing memory of pistachio comes from watching Laurel and Hardy argue about pistachio ice cream! Quite irrelevant to this recipe, but it sort of sets the tone. I hope this recipe brings that balance back and gives the pistachio some of the limelight.

60g unsalted butter, melted,
  plus extra for greasing
plain flour, for coating work
  surface
10 large sheets premade filo
  pastry, about 20 x 30cm
icing sugar, for decoration

for the filling

65g pistachio nuts, shelled and
  roughly chopped
50g almonds, finely chopped
25g granulated sugar
55g dark chocolate

Preheat the oven to 180°C/gas mark 4 and grease a couple of large baking trays. Prepare the filling by mixing all the ingredients together in one bowl.

Lightly flour a work surface and then cut all the filo sheets to make long, thin rectangular pieces, each measuring about 10 x 30cm. One at a time, brush the tops with melted butter and spoon some of the filling onto one end, ensuring that the pastry shows around the mixture in all directions.

Roll the pastry up lengthways and tuck the end underneath to create a parcel. Arrange all the parcels on the baking trays and bake for about 20 minutes.

When lightly browned, remove the filo parcels and cool on a wire rack before decorating with icing sugar.

chocolate and plum bakes

prep time, including chilling, 3 hours ✶ makes 8–12

These are beautifully balanced little bakes, with the sweet plums complementing the dark chocolate wonderfully. We have developed several recipes, but this one is a sweet chocolate pastry with a cream and plum filling. Use them as a pudding or as a very indulgent afternoon tea – if you ever have the time for such decadence!

for the base

170g dark chocolate, chopped
14g active dried yeast
100ml warm milk
large pinch of salt
6 tablespoons caster sugar
525g plain flour, plus extra for
  dusting
4 large eggs, beaten
320g butter, soft, plus extra
  for greasing

for the filling

480ml whole milk
4 large egg yolks

6 tablespoons sugar
3 tablespoons cornflour, sifted
pinch of salt
200g dark chocolate
2½ tablespoons unsalted
  butter, at room temperature
16 plums, pitted and quartered

special equipment

tartlet pans measuring 10cm
cutter 2cm larger than the
  tartlet pans
electric mixer with a dough
  hook
bain-marie or heatproof bowl

Grease the tartlet pans with butter. Place the chocolate in a bain-marie or a heatproof bowl over a pan of water that boiled 5 minutes earlier and is now off the heat and cooling. Stir occasionally until smooth.

Place the yeast and milk in a large bowl and beat lightly. Add the salt and sugar. Transfer to the bowl of an electric mixer and, using the dough hook attachment at a low speed, add the flour and eggs and beat for 1 minute. Once combined, continue mixing until smooth. Add the butter and mix for a further 3 minutes before finally adding the melted chocolate.

Cover with a clean cloth and leave in a warm place until the dough has doubled in volume, which will take 1–2 hours. When doubled, flip out the dough onto a floured surface and knock back the dough (by giving it a couple of firm punches and another quick knead) to get rid of any unwanted air pockets that have formed. You may need to repeat this a few times. Then refrigerate for 2–3 hours.

When cooled, roll out the dough to 1cm thick. Using your cutter, cut out rounds and line the buttered pans with the dough.

To make the chocolate filling, bring the milk to the boil in a pan. Whisk the yolks together in a bowl with the sugar, cornflour and salt, until thick.

Gradually add the milk to the egg and sugar mixture, whisking continuously, at first slowly, and then slightly faster. Put the pan over a medium heat. While still whisking vigorously and thoroughly around all edges of the pan, bring the mixture to the boil. Keep boiling and whisking for 1–2 minutes before removing from the heat.

Melt the chocolate, as before, in a bain-marie or a heatproof bowl over a pan of water that boiled 5 minutes earlier and is now off the heat and cooling. Stir occasionally until smooth.

Then whisk the chocolate into the filling. Let it stand for 5 minutes, before whisking in the butter, stirring until the cream is smooth and silky. Refrigerate for 20–30 minutes.

Preheat the oven to 180°C/gas mark 4. Spoon the pastry cream into the pastries and arrange the plum pieces on top. Cover the tarts with a clean cloth and leave in a warm place for about 15 minutes to rise.

When the tarts are risen, bake them for 15–20 minutes. Always let them cool before popping them out of the tartlet pans.

chocolate and apple tarte tatin

prep 30 minutes, plus 1 hour baking ✷ serves 4–8

This dish is apparently named after the Tatin sisters, who came up with the idea of caramelising the ingredients in butter and sugar and adding pastry before baking the tart in the oven, effectively upside down. No doubt this was the result of a cooking disaster, like so many great recipes. The apple works really well with the chocolate caramel, but try other options too. Don't restrict yourself to this recipe in the winter, although it does work well as a shield to fight the cold weather.

300g ready-made puff pastry
plain flour, for dusting
100g light muscovado sugar
80g unsalted butter, plus extra
  for greasing and glazing
75g dark chocolate, finely
  chopped

900g Braeburn apples, peeled
  and quartered

special equipment

8cm tarte tatin tin

Preheat the oven to 180°C/gas mark 4. Roll out the pastry on a floured surface to a disc 2.5cm larger than the tin. Set aside.

Cook the sugar and butter in the tin over a medium heat until a brown caramel is formed. Remove from the hob, add the chocolate and stir until melted into the caramel.

Arrange the apple quarters tightly in the tin, ensuring there are no gaps. Give this layer a brush with some melted butter. Bake for 30 minutes.

Remove the tin from the oven and place the pastry over the top, tucking in the overhanging pastry around the edges between the fruit and the tin. Prick a few holes in the top to allow the steam to escape during cooking.

Bake for about another 30 minutes, or until golden. Remove the tart and leave it to cool before removing it from the tin and serving it, apple side up.

variations

Use pear or banana to replace the apple.

TIP
You can cook the tart in advance and reheat it at 150°C/gas mark 2 for 20 minutes.

chocolate citrus tart

prep 1 hour, including baking ∗ serves 6

This recipe uses a biscuit and chocolate base and a tangy citrus filling. There is little else I can add, other than that you will want to make this recipe time after time.

250g Amaretti biscuits
50g dark chocolate, grated
75g unsalted butter, melted

120g unsalted butter, melted
120g ground hazelnuts
150g crème fraîche

for the filling

special equipment

4 large eggs
zest and juice of 2 lemons
zest and juice of 2 oranges
120g sugar

food-processor or blender
nice solid baking tray or flat
  dish about 20cm across

Preheat the oven to 180°C/gas mark 4. Finely crush the biscuits using a blender or food-processor and then add the chocolate and the melted butter so they begin to blend together.

Firmly press the mixture on the base of a solid baking tray to make a very well-compacted base. You may have to improvise with kitchen implements to help get the required pressure. Bake for 10 minutes.

Remove the tray from the oven and quickly work on the base again, pressing it down firmly.

To make the filling, beat the eggs in a bowl and whisk in the lemon and orange zest and juice with the sugar, butter and ground hazelnuts.

Pour the mixture on to the base and bake for about 25 minutes.

Leave the tart to cool before covering the top in crème fraîche straight from the fridge. Serve immediately.

This is one of the staples of any baker's armoury. The only change here is that the filling recipe follows the chocolate theme and some almonds have been added for extra body. Use ready-made puff pastry to keep things easy.

pithivier

prep 1 hour, plus 30 minutes baking * makes 8

70g dark chocolate, chopped
90g caster sugar
130g unsalted butter
25g unsweetened cocoa
  powder
150g almonds, finely ground
30g cornflour
3 large eggs, beaten, plus
  1 beaten egg for glazing

375g frozen puff pastry,
  thawed
plain flour, for dusting

special equipment

bain-marie or heatproof bowl
8cm cutter

Melt the chocolate in a bain-marie or a heatproof bowl over a pan of water that boiled 5 minutes earlier and is now off the heat and cooling. Stir occasionally until smooth.

Dissolve the sugar into the butter in a pan over a medium heat and then add the chocolate and stir until smooth. Mix the cocoa, almonds and cornflour together and then stir into the chocolate mixture. Finally, beat in the eggs until well combined.

Roll out the pastry on a floured surface into one rectangle about 0.5cm thick. Use an 8cm cutter to make about 16 rounds of pastry.

Spoon 1½–3 tablespoons of the filling into the centre of 8 of the pastry rounds, brush the remaining beaten egg around the edges of the pastry and enclose them with the remaining pastry rounds. Press firmly around the edges to ensure they are well sealed.

Place the pithiviers about 10cm apart on a baking tray lined with parchment paper and chill in the fridge for 15 minutes. Preheat the oven to 200°C/gas mark 6.

Remove the pithiviers from the fridge and brush the tops with egg. Using the point of a knife, make the traditional decoration of spiral lines, drawing from the top outwards and then scallop the edges.

Bake the pithiviers for 25–30 minutes until golden. Leave to cool on a wire rack.

3

Chilled & Frozen Desserts

The simple chocolate mousse is still sublime and always will be. However, in my view, we have come a long way with new flavours and techniques, and there are plenty of ideas for chilled desserts to explore. It's important to note that the quality of ingredients makes more of an impact to the taste, texture and colour of the recipes in this chapter than in any other chocolate category. This is no doubt down to the expectations of guests who will expect your chilled dessert to be something exquisite and delicate. Don't disappoint – buy quality ingredients and, crucially, don't get distracted by licking too many spoons during the preparations!

chocolate trifle

prep 45 minutes, plus 3 hours chilling ✳ serves 8

I have to admit to being a secret trifle hater. This is mainly due to various family Sunday lunches as a child when relations we didn't know would rock up bearing unwelcome gifts of layered custard and fruit – being a polite family we would be forced to eat them with a smile! This wonderful chocolate variation on the trifle theme makes a break with tradition to create a fabulous party food. The recipe contains a quick cheat in the form of a chocolate loaf cake, but you can make the cake from scratch using Helen's Banana and Chocolate Loaf recipe on page 44.

280g chocolate loaf cake, sliced
4 tablespoons seedless strawberry jam
1 tablespoon almond extract
250g mixed frozen red fruit, thawed
chocolate truffles, fresh cherries and fresh strawberries, to serve

for the chocolate custard

6 egg yolks
55g caster sugar

1 tablespoon cornflour
500ml whole milk
55g dark chocolate

for the topping

225ml double cream
1 tablespoon caster sugar
½ teaspoon vanilla essence

special equipment

bain-marie or heatproof bowl

Slice up the loaf cake and make cake sandwiches with the jam. Cut the slices into cubes and put them into a large serving bowl. Sprinkle with the almond extract and cover in the thawed fruit.

Make the custard by whisking the egg yolks and sugar in a heatproof bowl. Whisk the mixture until thick, before stirring in the cornflour.

Heat the milk in a pan until simmering and slowly and gradually pour the milk into the egg mixture, stirring continuously. When combined, return the mix to the milk pan and simmer, stirring constantly, until it thickens. Remove from the heat and leave for 5–10 minutes.

Meanwhile, melt the chocolate in a bain-marie or a heatproof bowl over a pan of water that boiled 5 minutes earlier and is now off the heat and cooling. Stir occasionally until smooth. Then stir the melted chocolate into the milk pan.

Pour the chocolate custard over the bowl of cake cubes and fruit and refrigerate for 3 hours until set.

Prepare the topping by whipping the cream to soft peaks before beating in the sugar and vanilla essence. Spoon the topping over the trifle before serving decorated with chocolate truffles, fresh cherries and strawberries.

variations

The alcohol can be left out or swapped for a little almond extract and the raspberry jam can be replaced with any number of other varieties.

TIP
It is best if the frozen fruit includes cherries because they add a little welcome sharpness.

orange and cardamom blancmange

prep 30 minutes, plus 2–3 hours chilling ✳ serves 8

Not the slightly odd English 1980s' synth band, but a quite delightful sweet dessert made from milk with a lovely texture and a powerful flavour.

250ml whole milk
250ml double cream
250g dark chocolate, chopped
6 large egg yolks
200g granulated sugar
2 teaspoons cornflour
2–3 drops orange essential oil
½ teaspoon ground cardamom

1½ teaspoons powdered gelatine
sunflower oil, for greasing
whipped cream and grated chocolate, to serve

special equipment

8 ramekins measuring 6–8 cm

Heat the milk and cream very gently in a pan over a medium heat so it doesn't simmer. Place the chocolate in a bowl, pour over the warm milk and cream mixture and stir until completely melted.

Beat the egg yolks, sugar and cornflour in a bowl until creamy. Slowly pour the chocolate mixture into the egg yolk mixture, mixing slowly and continuously. Add the orange drops and cardamom. Return the mixture to the pan on a low heat, beating constantly until thickened. Remove from the heat.

Dissolve the gelatine in a small bowl with about 2 tablespoons of boiling water. Stir this into the chocolate custard and leave it to cool.

Lightly oil the ramekins and divide the mixture equally between them. Cover and refrigerate for 3–4 hours.

When you are ready to serve, remove the chilled blancmanges from the ramekins. They should drop out with some gentle tapping and shaking, but they may need easing out gently. Decorate each one with a spoon of whipped cream and grated chocolate.

dolomite chocolate affair

prep 15 minutes, plus 8 hours chilling ∗ serves 10

This cold pudding was originally sampled in Italy on my one and only school skiing trip, a trip when half the class came back with a broken limb or two. Despite this, the trip was less memorable for terrible skiing in terrible clothes and terrible conditions, and more memorable for a very cool Human League album and this chocolate alternative to Christmas pudding! It was one of my first memories of really amazing chocolate puds and makes a fantastic alternative to the much-overrated traditional Christmas pudding.

butter, for greasing
100g mixed glacé fruit,
  chopped
65g sultanas
zest and juice of 1 orange
3 tablespoons orange juice
330g dark chocolate, chopped
3 tablespoons single cream
125g cream cheese
115g broken biscuits

125ml whipping cream,
  to serve
2 tablespoons Amaretto
  liqueur, to serve
25g dark chocolate, grated,
  to serve

special equipment

850ml pudding basin

Grease the pudding basin. Mix the fruit, sultanas, orange zest and juice in a large bowl. Gently melt the chocolate and cream in a pan and stir into the fruit mix, keeping a little chocolate and cream aside for the next step. Leave to cool.

Beat together the cream cheese and the reserved chocolate and cream. Mix this with the chocolate and fruit mix and stir in the broken biscuits. Now pour the entire contents into the prepared pudding basin and cover it with clingfilm. Refrigerate overnight.

When ready to serve, turn the pudding out onto a chilled serving plate. Lightly whip the whipping cream and liqueur and pour over the top of the pudding, sprinkling with grated chocolate to finish.

variations

The world of liqueurs is fascinating, and the Amaretto can be replaced with any number of different variants, including brandy. Of course it can be left out entirely if you have youngsters around!

nutcase: chestnut and chocolate terrine

prep 30 minutes, plus 8 hours chilling ✴ serves 6–8

The Nutcase was the very first truffle we produced using chestnut purée. Brighton was our first and only shop at the time the Nutcase was a smash hit. We only discontinued it because of a need to keep things changing. Maybe it's time for a comeback.

125g dark chocolate
220ml double cream
70ml dry sherry
250g biscuits, such as
  digestives
200g chestnut purée

unsweetened cocoa powder
  and icing sugar, to decorate

special equipment

400–500g loaf tin
bain-marie or heatproof bowl

Line the loaf tin with clingfilm. Melt the chocolate in a bain-marie or a heatproof bowl over a pan of water that boiled 5 minutes earlier and is now off the heat and cooling. Stir occasionally until smooth. Leave to cool.

Whip the cream to soft peaks and fold it into the cooled chocolate.

Pour the sherry into a dish and, taking a few biscuits at a time, dunk or soak them in the sherry (depending on how boozy you want the pudding to be). Arrange the biscuits in the loaf tin to create a thick base layer.

On top of the base, spread a layer of chocolate cream followed by a thin layer of dunked biscuits. Add a layer of chestnut purée and another biscuit layer.

Continue in this way, building up layers of alternate ingredients, finishing with a biscuit layer. Cover the whole thing with more clingfilm and refrigerate overnight.

When ready to serve, turn out and decorate with cocoa or icing sugar, or both.

white chocolate and summer fruit fools

prep 20 minutes, plus chilling ✳ serves 4

The dessert has everything going for it, and as a rather arty friend of ours once commented, they are impressionistic in appearance, although the exact meaning of this escapes me. In my own preferred language I would say that they are pretty and very indulgent, welcoming on even the hottest of lazy summer days.

100g white chocolate,
  chopped
80g raspberries
80g strawberries
80g blueberries
400g fromage frais

special equipment

bain-marie or heatproof bowl

Melt the white chocolate in a bain-marie or a heatproof bowl over a pan of water that boiled 5 minutes earlier and is now off the heat and cooling. You have to be especially careful not to burn white chocolate and this process will help to avoid this. Stir occasionally until smooth.

Keep back 4 pieces of each fruit for decoration, and roughly crush the remainder with a fork.

Mix the melted chocolate, fromage frais and crushed fruit and spoon the mixture into four glasses, creating a marbled effect. Decorate each portion with one of each of the remaining pieces of fruit and refrigerate until you are ready to serve.

sunshine

prep 1 hour, plus 30 minutes chilling ✶ serves 8

This is a smash hit in a glass, and the combination was entirely accidental – or, to be more accurate, it was born out of laziness. Because we hadn't made enough of any one mousse to cater for our family at Christmas, we decided to combine two mousses into one little glass. At the time we told everyone it was a 'strong orange mousse', as the kids would have pulled the house down if dessert had been for adults only! The name came from a fabulous orange truffle we make that simply was a little ball of sunshine!

4 oranges, in segments
grated chocolate, to decorate

for the chocolate mousse

330g dark chocolate
6 large egg whites
60g caster sugar
2 teaspoons powdered
  gelatine, dissolved in
  2 tablespoons boiling water
650ml heavy double cream,
  softly whipped

for the Grand Marnier mousse

4 large egg yolks
60g caster sugar
50ml orange juice, freshly
  squeezed
2 teaspoons powdered
  gelatine, dissolved in 2
  tablespoons of boiling water
70ml Grand Marnier
550ml heavy double cream,
  softly whipped

special equipment

bain-marie or heatproof bowl

To make the chocolate mousse, place the chocolate in a bain-marie or a heatproof bowl over a pan of water that boiled 5 minutes earlier and is now off the heat and cooling. Stir occasionally until smooth.

Whisk together the egg whites and sugar in a bowl until thick and creamy. Place the melted chocolate into a large bowl and stir in the dissolved gelatine. Now fold in the whipped cream and the eggs and sugar mixture (alternating between small amounts of each) until well combined and smooth. Set aside.

Make the Grand Marnier mousse by beating the egg yolks and sugar in a bowl until pale. Boil half the orange juice in a small pan before removing it from the heat and stirring in the gelatine until completely dissolved. Stir in the remaining orange juice and the liqueur. Gradually whisk the mixture into the egg yolks and sugar. Finally, fold in the cream.

To serve, place a few small orange segments in the base of each tall glass and spoon some chocolate mousse on top. Top this with more orange segments and more chocolate mousse so you have thin layers of each. Finish with a few more segments and a large amount of the Grand Marnier mousse. Decorate with grated chocolate and chill for 30 minutes before serving.

crunchy olive oil and chocolate mousse

prep 40 minutes, plus 8 hours chilling ✴ serves 6

Do I hear you scream in horror at the thought of olive oil and chocolate? Fear not, this is a combination that is used quite widely in Spanish recipes. We first tasted this at a great Spanish restaurant close to our first house in Putney.

for the mousse

200g dark chocolate
175ml light olive oil
5 eggs, separated
160g caster sugar
salt

for the praline

200g caster sugar
125g sesame seeds, lightly
   toasted

special equipment

bain-marie or heatproof bowl
6 x 6.5cm ramekins

Place the chocolate in a bain-marie or a heatproof bowl over a pan of water that boiled 5 minutes earlier and is now off the heat and cooling. Stir occasionally until smooth. When melted, stir in the olive oil.

Beat the egg yolks with 80g of the sugar in a bowl until fluffy. Now stir in the chocolate and oil. Whisk the egg whites in a bowl with a pinch of salt until stiff peaks start to form. Continue to whisk as you add another 80g of sugar in small batches. Finally, fold the egg whites into the chocolate.

Fill 6 ramekins with the mousse and refrigerate overnight.

Make the salt and sesame crunchy praline by putting the remaining 200g of sugar in a small pan over a low heat until the sugar has melted and turned golden brown. Stir in the sesame seeds and a pinch or two of salt before immediately spreading it out on a sheet of baking parchment using a spatula or palette knife.

When cooled, roughly break up the praline. Serve the mousse in the ramekins with a little crunchy praline on top.

chocolate mascarpone

prep 30 minutes, plus 2 hours chilling ∗ serves 8

We have cheated here by using ready-made meringues, but you could also use the recipe for Double Chocolate Meringues on page 27. There is no escaping the fact that this is sweet, but it is also the most fabulous summer pudding.

4 large egg yolks
200g granulated sugar
550g mascarpone cheese,
  softened
85ml sweet dessert wine
220g dark chocolate, chopped
6 tablespoons milk
10 ready-made meringues
grated dark chocolate,
  to decorate

special equipment

8 wide serving glasses

Beat the egg yolks and sugar in a bowl and then stir in the mascarpone and wine. Divide the mixture evenly between two bowls.

Melt the chocolate in a heatproof bowl over water that boiled 5 minutes ago and is now off the heat and cooling. Once melted, set aside to cool.

Mix the melted chocolate and the milk into one of the bowls so you end up with a plain mix and a chocolate mix.

Roughly break the meringues into the bases of the serving glasses and spoon on equal amounts of the plain and chocolate mixtures. If you are feeling artistic, swirl them gently to give a nice visual effect.

Refrigerate for at least 4 hours and decorate with grated chocolate.

variation

Use an interesting-flavoured chocolate bar, such as chilli and lime, for the grated decoration.

chocolate
mintmocha whirls

prep 15 minutes, plus 30 minutes chilling ✷ serves 4

I know it's a made-up word, but then every word is made up at some point, so perhaps we should think of 'mintmocha' as a new word. I could have gone the whole hog and called it 'chocomintimocha whirls', but that would have just been silly! Call them whatever you like, but in the end they are really good and you can knock together this surprisingly refreshing pudding in a jiffy.

300ml double cream
2 tablespoons icing sugar
150ml fromage frais
4 tablespoons coffee essence
(I like Camp Chicory &
Coffee essence, as the
chicory element is slightly
unusual and gives an
interesting taste)

175g dark chocolate
grated chocolate, to decorate
1–2 drops peppermint oil

special equipment

bain-marie or heatproof bowl
4 tall serving glasses

Whip the cream in a bowl until it forms soft peaks, then fold in the icing sugar and fromage frais. Transfer one third of the mixture into another bowl and mix in the coffee essence.

Melt the chocolate in a bain-marie or a heatproof bowl over a pan of water that boiled 5 minutes earlier and is now off the heat and cooling. Stir occasionally until smooth. Fold this into the other two thirds of the mixture with the peppermint oil.

Now place and 'swirl in' alternate small amounts of the mixes into tall glasses until they are full. Decorate with grated chocolate and chill for 30 minutes before serving.

cocoa mint soft jelly

prep 1 hour, plus 4 hours chilling * serves 8

This has become a refreshing classic in our household. Simplified from a stunning dish we had in a beautiful restaurant in Montpellier, this is an impressive dessert that we have served many times, in fact almost every New Year's Eve when our regular visitors at this time of year never seem to bore of it.

for the mint sorbet

400g caster sugar
20ml mint liqueur
4 tablespoons green food
  colouring

for the cocoa jelly

8 sheets gelatine
50ml milk

300g caster sugar
170g unsweetened cocoa
  powder
1 small bunch fresh mint
300g dark mint chocolate,
  minimum 70 per cent cocoa
  solids, optional

To make the mint sorbet, bring 3 litres of water to the boil in a pan with the sugar. Remove the pan from the heat when the syrup is thick and leave to cool.

Add the mint liqueur and the green food colouring to the syrup before freezing it overnight. For a smooth result, keep removing it from the freezer and break up the forming ice crystals with a fork to make smaller flakes.

To make the cocoa jelly, soften the sheets of gelatine in a bowl of cold water.

Bring the milk to the boil in a pan and add the cocoa. Drain the gelatine sheets and add them to the cocoa milk, mixing until well blended and smooth.

Boil 100ml of water with the sugar. When the syrup is thick, add it to the jelly. Strain the mixture and put it in the fridge for 4 hours.

If you want to make chocolate-coated mint leaves to decorate, temper the mint chocolate following the instructions on page 12. Dip the mint leaves into the tempered chocolate and set them aside to set. Alternatively, you can just use plain mint leaves to garnish.

When ready to serve, pour the cocoa jelly into serving glasses and cover with the mint sorbet. Decorate with mint leaves or chocolate mint leaves and serve.

chocolate and mint zabaione

prep 30 minutes ∗ serves 4–8

This wonderful quick and easy pudding broadly follows the Italian method. We have skipped the sweet wine in this recipe, however, because we use it for family lunches where we find it best to keep both young and old off the boozy stuff for as long as possible! We serve this over vanilla ice cream, although it is also a success on its own.

200g dark chocolate
1 peppermint tea bag
100ml milk
4 egg yolks
100g sugar
vanilla ice cream, to serve

special equipment

bain-marie or heatproof bowl

Melt the chocolate in a bain-marie or a heatproof bowl over a pan of water that boiled 5 minutes earlier and is now off the heat and cooling. Stir occasionally until smooth.

Add 100g of boiling water to the peppermint tea bag and brew for 5 minutes before discarding the tea bag. Meanwhile gently boil the milk in another pan. Take the milk off the heat and leave to cool for 2 minutes.

Beat the egg yolks with the sugar in a bowl until airy, and put in a pan. Pour the milk and the tea slowly and gently over the yolks, heating them gently over a low heat, stirring continuously. Now add the melted chocolate and bring the mixture to a high simmer.

Place a ball of vanilla ice cream in each serving glass before pouring the mixture over and serving.

variations

25ml brandy can be added when adding the melted chocolate to the mixture.

chocolate ice cream bombe

prep 1 hour, plus 24 hours freezing (if not using
an ice-cream maker) ★ serves 8–10

**You need to make two different ice creams for this dessert but it results
in a very striking summer pudding.**

for the dark chocolate
ice cream

2 eggs, plus 2 egg yolks
100g caster sugar
250g dark chocolate, chopped
  roughly
290ml single cream
310ml double cream

for the white chocolate
ice cream

155ml whole milk
150g white chocolate,
  chopped roughly

60g caster sugar
310ml double cream

unsweetened cocoa powder,
  to dust

special equipment

ice-cream maker (if you have
  one) or a rounded pudding
  bowl about 1.5 litres in
  capacity and lined with
  clingfilm

To make the dark chocolate ice cream, beat the eggs, egg yolks and sugar in a
heatproof bowl. At the same time, put the chocolate and single cream in a heavy-
based pan and heat very gently until the chocolate melts, and then turn up the
heat a little, stirring constantly, until the mixture is close to boiling.

Pour the hot chocolate and cream over the egg mix in the heatproof bowl and
set the whole thing over a pan of simmering water so the steam heats the mixture
above. Keep this on the heat until the mixture begins to thicken, which should
take 5–10 mins. Leave to cool.

Whisk the double cream until thick and fold it into the cooled chocolate mix.

If you are using an ice-cream maker, place the mixture in the machine and follow
the manufacturer's instructions.

If you are not using an ice-cream maker, put the mixture into a suitable container
and place in the freezer. Remove after about 1 hour and beat it with a fork. Then
place the mixture into the clingfilm-lined rounded pudding bowl.

Put the bowl in the freezer and then, about every 2 hours, remove the mixture
and beat it vigorously to break down the ice crystals. If you leave it, the ice cream
will be very coarse and crunchy.

Repeat the above stage at least 3 or 4 more times. Leave the ice cream overnight in the freezer. Move it into the fridge when you are ready to start making the white chocolate ice cream.

To make the white chocolate ice cream, put half the milk and the chocolate in a bain-marie or a heatproof bowl over a pan of water that boiled 5 minutes earlier and is now off the heat and cooling, heating it very gently to melt the chocolate. You have to be especially careful not to burn white chocolate. Stir occasionally until smooth.

Melt the sugar and the remainder of the milk together in a pan and then leave the contents to cool completely. Once cool, mix with the white chocolate mixture.

Whip the cream until it starts to form soft peaks and fold it into the chocolate mixture.

Take your dark chocolate ice cream out of the fridge, spoon out a big hole in the middle of the dark chocolate ice cream (you can put this removed ice cream back in the freezer and save it for another time). Pour the cooled white chocolate mix into the hole you've created. Put the bombe in the freezer for another 3–6 hours.

When ready to serve, dip the bowl in warm water to release the ice cream. Be careful not to allow water on the ice cream. Dry the bowl and turn it out on to a serving plate. Dust with cocoa powder to serve.

frozen cappuccino

prep 30 minutes, plus 8 hours freezing ✷ serves 10

Coffee is possibly my second favourite food addiction after chocolate, but unlike chocolate it was something I got a taste for quite late in life. I would like to call it part of a growing sophistication, but Helen suggests that I never really grew up. Anyway, this recipe brings both my food loves together in one potent package.

4 large eggs, separated
110g caster sugar
480ml double cream, firmly
  whipped
3 tablespoons good-quality
  instant coffee mixed with
  1 tablespoon boiling water

70g dark chocolate, finely
  grated
unsweetened cocoa powder,
  for dusting

special equipment

10 double espresso cups

Beat the egg yolks and half the sugar in a bowl until pale and creamy.

Beat the egg whites and the remaining sugar in another bowl until soft peaks form, and then fold the whites into the yolks and sugar with a wooden spoon. Finally fold in the whipped cream, followed by the coffee mixture and the finely grated chocolate.

Take 10 double espresso cups and wrap each one tightly in parchment paper to create a 2cm lip around the top. This is slightly fiddly but worth spending some time on. Alternatively, use glass cups as we have in the photo. Now pour in the coffee mixture to just below the top of the paper and place the cups in the freezer overnight.

When ready to serve, carefully peel off the paper and dust each one with cocoa powder to create 10 amazing little chocolate coffee hits!

chocolate alaska

prep 40 minutes, plus 3–6 hours freezing time ∗ serves 8

Anyone of a certain age will remember 007 being presented with a Bombe Surprise at the end of *Diamonds are Forever*. While that certainly dates the origins of this elegant recipe, our variation brings it right up to date, and fit for any elegant entertaining with or without a member of Her Majesty's Secret Service present! This remains one of the top puds of all time in our house.

for the praline ice cream

60g hazelnuts, cleaned and
  finely chopped
110g caster sugar
500ml (one standard-size tub)
  vanilla ice cream, softened
500ml (one standard-size tub)
  chocolate ice cream, softened

for the meringue

8 large egg whites
410g caster sugar

special equipment

8 individual 100–140g
  pudding bowls
kitchen blow torch (if you
  have one)

Begin by making the praline. Preheat the oven to 200°C/gas mark 6. Lightly toast the hazelnuts on a baking tray lined with parchment paper, until golden but not burnt. Watch them carefully for 5–10 minutes. Remove the tray from the heat and leave the nuts to cool.

Bring the sugar and 500ml water to a boil in a heavy pan over medium heat and simmer until the mixture is a light golden colour. Remove the mixture from the heat and pour it over the hazelnuts on their baking tray. Leave the praline to set.

Once cool, chop the set praline into pieces before folding it into the softened vanilla ice cream. Put this back in the freezer to harden. This is our hazelnut praline ice cream.

Chill the pudding bowls in the freezer for 15 minutes. Take them out one at a time and half fill each one with soft chocolate ice cream, before adding the harder praline ice cream to the centre of the chocolate ice cream so it 'pushes' into the centre leaving chocolate ice cream around the outside. Level the bowls off and place them back in the freezer for 1 hour.

When hard, remove the bombes by briefly dipping the base of the bowl into hot water to release them. Place the individual bombes back in the freezer as you go.

To make the meringue, beat the egg whites and sugar until stiff peaks start to form. When ready to serve, work quickly on one bombe at a time so they do not soften. Completely cover the bombes with a delicate layer of the meringue mix before gently browning each one with a kitchen blow torch, if you have one – if not, you could do this under the grill.

arctic soufflés

prep 35 minutes, plus 24 hours freezing ✶ serves 6

Because these soufflés can be prepared 24 hours in advance, and they look as amazing as they taste, this is one pudding we use more often than any other. It's a real winner every time. This version has coffee and chicory essence, but this ingredient can be left out if you want to cater for children.

100g dark chocolate, chopped roughly
6 tablespoons Camp Chicory & Coffee essence (available from most supermarkets)
4 eggs, separated
120g icing sugar

250ml double cream
30g milk chocolate shavings, to decorate

special equipment
6 x 6.5cm ramekins
bain-marie or heatproof bowl

Take the ramekins and tightly wrap them in silver foil, but make the height twice the height of the ramekin – this creates an area for the soufflé to 'rise' into.

Melt the chocolate in a bain-marie or a heatproof bowl over a pan of water that boiled 5 minutes earlier and is now off the heat and cooling. Stir occasionally until smooth. Mix in the chicory and coffee essence.

Beat the egg yolks and icing sugar in a bowl until thick, before whisking in the melted chocolate. Whisk the cream in another bowl until thick.

Whisk the egg whites until stiff peaks start to form in another clean bowl. Fold the egg whites into the chocolate along with the whipped cream. Spoon this light mixture into the ramekins, filling them to the top. Freeze for 24 hours.

Remove the ramekins from the freezer 10 minutes before serving. Remove the foil and decorate the soufflés with grated milk chocolate.

three-minute delight: cocoa, mango and chilli sorbet

prep 15 minutes, plus 3–4 hours freezing ∗ serves 4

This takes three minutes to make... but hold on, it takes a few hours to freeze and there is more time involved if you don't have an ice-cream maker! But please give it a go because it is sweet, oozes cocoa and has a hint of hidden danger. When we stopped making our Lime Pickle at Montezuma's there was an outcry from our customers like no other we had experienced, and this sorbet was where the idea for the pickle all started.

200g unsweetened cocoa powder
2 fresh mangoes, chopped and blended into a purée
very small pinch of ground chilli
350g caster sugar
1 litre mineral or filtered water (gives better flavour)

brandy snaps, to serve

special equipment

ice-cream maker, if you have one

Mix the cocoa, mango purée, chilli and sugar in a heavy-based pan and heat on low. Gradually pour in the mineral or filtered water, whisking continuously so the mixture stays smooth. Remove the mixture from the heat as soon as it begins to boil and leave to cool.

If you have an ice-cream maker, pour the mixture into the ice-cream maker, set to sorbet, churn and leave it until ready. (This is the easy method.) The ice-cream maker continually scrapes the ice so it does the hard work for you, although arguably gives a less rewarding sorbet than the alternative method below.

If you don't have an ice-cream maker, place your mixture in the freezer (ideally in a metal bowl) and after the first couple of hours whisk it regularly to ensure it doesn't freeze with large ice crystals – use an electric whisk if you have one to smash those ice crystals into nano-particles! (This is the harder method that will keep you much fitter.)

Before serving, place the dessert cups in the freezer for an hour. Take the cups and sorbet out together and scoop the sorbet into the cups. This is great served with old-fashioned brandy snaps.

chilli and lime chocolate sorbet

prep 15 minutes, plus 4½ hours freezing ✱ serves 8

If this combination of flavours sounds too much for any sane person, let me reassure you it works brilliantly as long as the chilli is subtle and balances against the fruity lime and chocolate. The use of spice in chocolate needs to be balanced and interesting while also allowing the chocolate to dominate. This is more of a 'warm and cool' experience than the expected 'hot and cold' shock.

500g dark chocolate, finely chopped
small pinch of ground chilli (this needs to be finely ground and only use a pinch!)
400g granulated sugar
juice of 2 limes

special equipment

bain-marie or heatproof bowl
ice-cream maker, if you have one

Melt the chocolate in a bain-marie or a heatproof bowl over a pan of water that boiled 5 minutes earlier and is now off the heat and cooling. Stir occasionally until smooth, before adding the chilli evenly to the chocolate.

Put the sugar, lime juice and 1 litre of water in a pan over a medium heat and stir until the sugar has dissolved. Stir in the melted chocolate before removing from the heat. Leave to cool to room temperature before chilling for 30 minutes.

If you have an ice-cream maker, place the mixture in the machine and follow the manufacturer's instructions.

If you don't have an ice-cream maker, place the mix in a metal bowl and put it in the freezer. After about 2 hours, when the mixture has just begun to set, whisk it vigorously with an electric beater or by hand, until the ice crystals are broken down and it is creamy and smooth.

Repeat the above stage at least 3 or 4 more times until the sorbet is thick and smooth. The more you whisk and repeat the process, the smoother it will be.

variation

Just about anything you can freeze in the water or mix with the chocolate will technically work, so get experimenting with wild combinations.

4

Warm Puddings

It is probably fair to classify many of these recipes as part of that soft and spongy world we call comfort food. You shouldn't feel the need to restrict yourself, however, to eating these in the winter – just don't plan a half marathon 30 minutes afterwards, unless it's downhill on a skateboard.

clafoutis

prep 15 minutes, and 50 minutes baking ∗ serves 6

This wonderful wobbly dessert uses succulent cherries and originates in the Massif Central region of France. It is one of those core recipes that every family should experiment with to come up with their very own 'secret family recipe'! As you may have guessed, ours contains chocolate.

butter, for greasing
500g black cherries, stoned,
  plus extra to serve
3 eggs
50g caster sugar
50g self-raising flour
20g unsweetened cocoa
  powder

150ml double cream
300ml whole milk
icing sugar, for decoration
single cream, to serve

special equipment

23cm ovenproof dish

Preheat the oven to 190°C/gas mark 5 and grease the dish. Place the cherries in the dish as tightly as possible, keeping a few aside for decoration.

Make the batter by whisking together the eggs and the sugar in a bowl. Sift the flour and cocoa in a bowl and add this to the egg mixture. Beat the mixture until smooth and then add the double cream and milk.

Pour the batter over the cherries and bake for about 50 minutes, or until the clafoutis is golden brown and slightly risen. Check it is set by inserting a skewer into the middle and seeing if it comes out clean. Decorate the clafoutis with a few fresh cherries and lightly dust with some icing sugar. Serve with single cream.

variations

Replace the cherries with other fresh fruits, such as peaches or plums.

TIP To intensify the taste of the cherries, take some very ripe cherries, stalks and all, and soak them in a bowl of ice cubes. The cherries will swell a little but the taste intensifies considerably.

orange and geranium chocolate souffle

prep: 25 minutes, plus 13 minutes baking ✶ serves: 6

There are a thousand marginally different methods for making a soufflé. They share many characteristics but all have one common instruction, which I failed to understand the first time I made one. Don't open the door while it's cooking! This soufflé has the added twist of using our Orange and Geranium Chocolate. You could, of course, add your own flavours or oils, but the balance of flavour in the bar is perfect to give this a very subtle and interesting twist... that is about the only sales pitch in this book!

300g Montezuma's Orange
  and Geranium Chocolate
6 eggs
60ml whole milk
40g cornflour
pinch of salt
160g caster sugar
1 knob of butter

1 tablespoon flour
icing sugar or unsweetened
  cocoa powder, to serve

special equipment

bain-marie or heatproof bowl
soufflé ramekin

Preheat the oven to 180°C/gas mark 4. Melt the chocolate in a bain-marie or a heatproof bowl over a pan of water that boiled 5 minutes earlier and is now off the heat and cooling. Stir occasionally until smooth.

While the chocolate is melting, separate the eggs. Set 4 of the egg whites aside to use in another recipe, so that you have 2 egg whites and 6 yolks for your soufflé. Then add the milk and cornflour to a pan and bring to the boil, stirring constantly. As soon as it boils, remove from the heat and blend in the melted chocolate followed by the egg yolks, one at a time.

Add a tiny pinch of salt to the egg whites and beat them until stiff peaks start to form, at the same time adding the sugar gradually.

Gently fold the beaten egg whites into the chocolatey mix with a wooden spoon. Butter and flour the soufflé ramekin and fill it halfway with the chocolate mixture.

Set your timer to 13 minutes and put the ramekin in the oven. You have been warned – don't open the door until the 13 minutes are up!

Serve the soufflé immediately with a dusting of icing sugar or cocoa.

banana and chocolate galettes

prep 1 hour, plus 1 hour baking and resting ✱ serves 8

The galette is a versatile and easily adapted crusty bake, but this banana and chocolate version was sourced from a traditional pear recipe we sampled in western France on a family holiday. The banana is sweeter and was preferred by our kids at the time – they thought hot pears were weird while hot banana was perfectly normal. For this recipe we make the pastry, but you can buy it premade.

450g plain flour, plus extra for dusting
75g unsweetened cocoa powder
80g caster sugar
½ teaspoon salt
375g unsalted butter, cubed
6 bananas, peeled and sliced thinly at a 45 degree angle

Mix the flour, cocoa, sugar and salt in a large bowl before adding the butter and mixing gently.

Create a well in the mixture and pour in 150ml ice-cold water. Gently mix all the ingredients together to make a lovely dough, to which you can gradually add another 150ml ice-cold water. Don't worry if the butter is still visible in the dough.

Roll out the dough on a floured work surface to make a rectangle measuring about 15 x 30cm. Create a three-layered dough rectangle by folding one long side to the middle and then the other long side over the top.

Turn the rectangle 90 degrees, roll out to the original size and repeat the three layered trick. Cover and refrigerate for 30 minutes before repeating the entire process and chilling again.

Repeat the entire process yet again and then leave the dough to relax for 20 minutes.

Preheat the oven to 200°C/gas mark 6. Roll the pastry into a square about 1cm thick and use a 9cm pastry cutter to make pastry circles.

Place the pastry circles on a baking tray and decorate each one with slices of banana, leaving a border around the edge.

Bake the galettes until they are crisp and well puffed and the banana is beginning to brown – this will take about 15–20 minutes. Cool them on wire racks before serving warm.

salted caramel puddings

prep 30 minutes, plus overnight freezing and
40 minutes baking ∗ serves 6

The idea here was to take another classic chocolate pudding recipe and twist it around a little with some added caramel and a hint of salt. The subtle saltiness is important and adds a lovely complexity to what could otherwise be an over-sweet pudding.

6 tablespoons dulce de leche
  (or caramel)
135g unsalted butter, softened
  and at room temperature,
  plus extra for greasing
110g caster sugar
2 large eggs
170g self-raising flour
120ml sour cream
6 pinches salt (one pinch for
  each ramekin)

2–3 tablespoons unsweetened
  cocoa powder, plus extra for
  coating and dusting
single cream, to serve

special equipment

ice cube tray
6 x 6.5cm ramekins

Pour the dulce de leche or caramel into 6 empty moulds in an ice cube tray. Place in the freezer overnight.

Preheat the oven to 180°C/gas mark 4. Take the ramekins and wipe them in soft butter before coating them with cocoa.

Beat the butter and sugar in a bowl until pale and creamy. Add one egg at a time to the mixture, beating continuously. Now fold in half the flour, the sour cream, the other half of the flour, the salt and the cocoa.

Half fill each ramekin with the mixture and place one frozen dulce de leche square in the centre. Cover this with the remaining mixture.

Now bake the puds until springy, which will take about 30–40 minutes. When they are ready, leave the puddings to cool for 5 minutes before turning them out on to the serving plates. Dust with cocoa and serve with single cream.

spiced chocolate beer fritters

prep 60 minutes, plus overnight freezing ∗ makes around 30

Whilst I won't claim that these are the healthiest choice, they are fun and tasty and can be enjoyed in moderation! They are best combined with a little spice or a little salt, but can be made without either (in which case do leave the salt in the batter mix).

for the chocolate balls

200g dark chocolate
150ml whipping cream
generous pinch ground chilli
  or fine salt (I have tried both
  and it didn't really work)
unsweetened cocoa powder,
  to coat

for the batter

130g plain flour
1 tablespoon cornflour
1 tablespoon vegetable oil
very generous pinch salt
1 egg, beaten, and 1 egg white
100ml beer of your choice
25g caster sugar
vegetable oil, for frying

special equipment

bain-marie or heatproof bowl
piping bag (optional)

Make the chocolate balls by melting the chocolate in a bain-marie or a heatproof bowl over a pan of water that boiled 5 minutes earlier and is now off the heat and cooling.

Heat the cream in another pan until simmering and pour it over the chocolate. Stir the mixture gently until smooth, adding the chilli or the salt. Chill until firm.

Remove the mixture from the fridge and either pipe or spoon 30 small and neat large marble-sized amounts on to a baking tray. Put the baking tray in the fridge to firm up the balls before rolling each one in your hands to make it round (cold hands are needed for this). Roll the balls in cocoa before freezing overnight.

The next day, make the batter by sifting both flours into a big bowl. Make a well in the middle and add the oil, salt and whole beaten egg. Blend until smooth. Gradually add the beer, mixing constantly to keep the mixture smooth.

In a separate bowl, whisk the egg white to soft peaks and then whisk in the sugar to make it shiny before adding this to the batter.

Heat 4cm oil in a deep, heavy bottomed pan to around 200°C. (If you don't have a thermometer, you can do the bread cube test. Simply drop a small cube of bread into the oil. If it sizzles and turns golden, the oil is hot enough.) Take a couple of chocolate balls at a time from the freezer, coat them in the batter and, using a slotted spoon, deep-fry them in the oil until golden brown. Remove and dry on kitchen paper. Repeat until all the balls are done.

Serve the fritters warm or cold.

pears belle hélène

prep 1 hour ✳ serves 4

This recipe was probably created by the French chef Georges Auguste Escoffier and is likely to have been named after Helen, Queen of Sparta. Two uncertain elements, but what is certain is that our simplified version makes it quick and easy and doesn't stint on quality.

4 ripe pears (Comice pears are always a favourite)
50g caster sugar
1 vanilla pod, split open
1 litre milk
200g unsweetened cocoa powder
good-quality ice cream, to serve
toasted almonds, to decorate (optional)

To prepare the pears, peel and core the fruit. Place the pears upright and side by side in a saucepan (they need to be a snug fit in the pan so they stay upright).

Put enough water in the pan to cover the pears. Once you've added the water, take the pears out and set aside for a moment. Add the sugar and vanilla pod. Bring the contents of the pan to the boil and simmer for 5 minutes before returning the pears to the pan. Simmer until the pears are tender but not falling apart (they need to keep their shape). Take the pan off the heat and allow the contents to cool.

Now make the runny chocolate sauce. Pour the milk into a blender or food-processor and whizz for 15–20 minutes until you can't stand the noise any longer! Add the milk to a pan and bring to the boil, and then add the cocoa gradually, whisking continuously. Reduce the heat to a very gentle simmer and continue whisking for 5 minutes until the chocolate mixture is thick.

To serve, place a generous amount of ice cream on a serving plate, position the pears on the plate and pour over the hot sauce. Toasted almonds are a great decorative addition.

chocolate bread and butter pudding

prep 30 mins, plus up to 1 hour baking ∗ serves 6–8

There are one or two very well-known recipes for this, particularly Delia Smith's recipe, which is very hard to beat. Our twist on this has always been to use fruit bread, still a few days old, but the added texture is great in this winter pudding.

100g dark chocolate
575ml whole milk
150ml double cream
65g unsalted butter, plus extra
  for greasing
12 triangles fruit bread (sides
  about 8cm)
3 eggs

40g caster sugar
1 tablespoon demerara sugar
single cream, to serve

special equipment

shallow, ovenproof dish
  measuring 20 x 20cm.

Preheat the oven to 160°C/gas mark 3 and grease the ovenproof dish with butter.

Heat the chocolate, milk and cream gently and slowly in a pan until the chocolate has melted.

Butter the fruit bread on both sides and arrange the slices standing up in the dish.

Whisk the eggs and caster sugar into the chocolate mix and pour the mixture over the bread in the dish. Leave the bread to soak up the mixture for 15 minutes. It may need dunking from time to time.

Sprinkle the demerara sugar over the bread.

Bake for 45–60 minutes – you will get better results if you sit the dish in a big roasting tray filled with hot water. This will help prevent the lovely chocolate custard doing the curdle trick and spoiling the party. Serve the bread and butter pudding with cold single cream.

chocolate lava cakes

prep 20 minutes, plus 15 minutes baking ✳
makes 8 little cakes

**These individual little chocolate cakes are sublime, especially when they
are moist, rich and served with custard.**

130g dark chocolate
110g unsalted butter, cubed,
 plus extra for greasing
4 eggs
140g granulated sugar
55g plain flour
vanilla custard, to serve

special equipment

8 individual 6cm moulds
bain-marie or heatproof bowl

Grease the individual moulds with butter and line each one with parchment paper,
making sure that it sticks about 1–2cm up above the mould.

Melt the chocolate in a bain-marie or a heatproof bowl over a pan of water that
boiled 5 minutes earlier and is now off the heat and cooling. Stir occasionally until
smooth. Mix in the butter gradually.

Whisk together the eggs and sugar in a bowl until thick and creamy and add this
to the chocolate mix. Sift in the flour. Stir the mixture until just combined and
then stop. Don't overstir.

Pour the mixture into the moulds and bake them for 10–12 minutes. Serve the
cakes immediately with vanilla custard.

chocolate fruit crumble

prep 10 minutes, plus 45 minutes baking ✳ serves 4

We started down the slippery slope of encouraging one of our daughters to eat fruit by combining it with chocolate. Probably not a great parenting technique, but it must have worked because she does now eat lots of fruit without chocolate. It also set a precedent that contributed largely to the creation of this book so that other parents can share the joy of food bribery! The chocolate crumble topping makes an already great dessert truly outstanding.

350g canned apricots, in natural juice
400g cooking apples, peeled and thickly sliced
100g plain flour
6 tablespoons butter, cubed, with extra for greasing
65g porridge oats

4 tablespoons caster sugar
120g milk or dark chocolate, roughly chopped
cream or ice cream, to serve

special equipment

30cm ovenproof dish

Preheat the oven to 180°C/gas mark 4 and grease the ovenproof dish.

Combine the apricots and apple slices in the dish.

To make the crumble, sift the flour into a large bowl and rub in small cubes of butter with your fingers until the mixture begins to resemble breadcrumbs. Now stir in the oats, sugar and chocolate.

Sprinkle the crumble over the fruit and gently smooth it over without squashing the fruit. Bake for about 40–45 minutes until the crumble is golden brown. Serve warm with cream or ice cream.

variations

Replace the canned apricots with other canned fruit, such as pears. You can also use fresh fruit rather than canned fruit, in which case add a couple of tablespoons of orange juice.

TIP
Try adding ground almonds to the flour (about a third works well) when making the crumble.

ricotta, chocolate and orange turnovers

prep 45 minutes, including chilling, plus
25 minutes baking ∗ makes 12

Sweet and soft inside and crunchy and brown on the outside. Not me, but these lovely turnovers with chocolate and ricotta. The orange adds a little citrus burst to an otherwise perfect afternoon treat.

240g ricotta cheese, drained
80g granulated sugar
2 drops essential orange oil
2 large egg yolks
1 tablespoon vanilla extract
2 tablespoons plain flour, plus
  extra for dusting
50g crystallised orange sticks,
  finely chopped
1 tablespoon unsweetened
  cocoa powder

70g raisins
70g dark chocolate, finely
  chopped
360g premade puff pastry
1 large egg, lightly beaten,
  for glazing
40g demerara sugar

special equipment

food-processor

Preheat the oven to 200°C/gas mark 6 and line two baking trays with parchment paper.

Smooth the ricotta for 10 seconds in a food-processor before adding the sugar, essential oil, egg yolks and vanilla extract and mixing for another 20 seconds on a slow speed. Transfer to a large bowl.

Mix together the flour, chopped orange sticks and cocoa and then fold into the ricotta mixture. Add the raisins and chopped chocolate before chilling for 30 minutes.

Because the puff pastry is premade, hide the packet and then place the pastry on a floured work surface. Dust the surface with flour and roll the pastry out into a 35 x 45cm rectangle about 0.5cm thick. Trim if neccessary to make sure it is neat.

Cut the pastry into 12 squares and neatly place 2 tablespoons of the filling onto each square. Brush the egg around the edges and fold one corner diagonally to the opposite corner. Ensure you press down firmly around the edges to join the sides.

Lay out the prepared turnovers on the baking trays, brush them with the beaten egg and sprinkle them with demerara sugar. Bake for about 25 minutes, until golden. Cool on a wire rack. Enjoy with friends – or alone in a darkened room.

chocolate brioche with orange and ginger

prep 1 hour (no-kneading method) or 2 hours (kneading method), plus up to 50 minutes baking ∗ serves 4 cyclists or 8 pedestrians

We have spent many holidays in France camping or self-catering while exploring the Alps or the Pyrénées by bike, and on occasions we have 'accidentally' happened across the Tour de France. This short and apparently innocuous preamble provides ample ammunition to excuse the excessive consumption of local delicacies in and around these beautiful villages.

Astonishingly, it was only eight years ago when I first got a taste for brioche. It was due to a fabulous bakery in Bagnères-de-Bigorre where they made exquisitely rich chocolate brioche. After much playing with recipes this was about as close as I could get, but in all honesty the best results are achieved if you have just cycled over the Col du Tourmalet!

I have never been a fan of 'no-knead' bread or brioche. I find the results indifferent, simply because the kneading really does work, and gives bread and brioche that lovely 'stretching' feel. Having said that, this recipe does have a no-knead option, which does work, and tastes almost as good as anything kneaded. Eat this alone as a warm pudding, or toasted with butter or possibly chocolate spread!

375g flour (500g for the no-knead method), plus extra for dusting
30g sugar (50g for the no-knead method)
10g salt
12g active dried yeast (1–2g for the no-knead method)
100g crystallised ginger
100g crystallised orange peel

150g dark chocolate, minimum 73 per cent cocoa solids, broken into chunks
4 large eggs, beaten
250g unsalted butter, plus extra for greasing
60ml whole milk

special equipment

450g loaf tin

There are two methods for this recipe – one requires kneading and the other doesn't. Choose your method depending on how much energy and time you have. Both will produce similar results, but the kneading method will improve the gluten content of the brioche, meaning a springy and elastic dough and, eventually, a more even brioche.

Continued overleaf

No-kneading method

Preheat the oven to 180°C/gas mark 4. Grease the loaf tin with butter.

Mix all the dry ingredients in one bowl and all the wet ingredients (except the milk) in another bowl, whisking in the butter to the wet ingredients last.

Combine the wet and dry ingredients, ensuring there are no lumps, and let the mixture rest for several hours under a tea-towel until it doubles in size.

Fold in the edges of the mix, working around the bowl several times (we won't call this kneading) – keep your hands cool and slightly damp! Flip the dough over and let it rest overnight at room temperature before repeating the process. Now go to the instructions 'for both methods'.

Kneading method

Preheat the oven to 180°C/gas mark 4. Grease the loaf tin with butter.

Mix all the dry ingredients in a bowl, add the eggs and form the mixture into a ball. Knead the mixture on a lightly floured board for about 10–15 minutes, until it is smooth and comes away from the board cleanly.

Add the butter and knead for about another 10 minutes until the dough is smooth and very elastic – be prepared for an initial mess before the dough comes together.

Put the dough back in the bowl and wait for about 1 hour until it has doubled in size. Now take the dough out again, punch it down and put it back for another hour's rest until it has doubled in size again.

For both methods

Put the dough into the buttered tin, brush it with the milk and bake in the middle of the oven for 10 minutes. Turn the oven down to 160°C/gas mark 3 and bake for a further 20–40 minutes. The brioche should end up a nice dark brown colour – use the old-fashioned 'tap the loaf with a finger and listen for a hollow sound' technique to test it. You can't walk away and leave this one, so stay close to the oven and keep an eye on it!

dark chocolate risotto

prep 30 minutes ★ serves 4

Don't be scared by the word 'risotto' and all the mysteries of its preparation. This one takes barely 30 minutes, and everyone will be amazed at your technical skills. First developed in Sicily, the risotto has come a long away and this slightly spicy dessert version is a modern-day delight.

3 tablespoons unsweetened
 cocoa powder
100g sugar
¼ teaspoon ground cinnamon
900ml whole milk
150g risotto rice

zest of 3 oranges
100g dark chocolate
75g candied lemon peel,
 chopped
tiny pinch of chilli powder
single cream, to serve

Put the cocoa, sugar and cinnamon in a small bowl and add 4 tablespoons of the milk. Blend together before adding another 4 tablespoons of milk.

Put the rice in a medium pan and stir in the cocoa-flavoured milk, the remaining milk and the orange zest. Slowly bring to the boil before reducing the heat. Cover and lightly simmer for 20 minutes.

The rice should now be tender and creamy. If the mixture has dried out too much, add a little extra hot milk.

Stir in the chocolate until it has completely melted. Then add the lemon peel and a pinch of chilli. Serve in four warmed bowls with single cream.

chocolate rice pudding

prep 30 minutes * serves 6

When we were kids, rice pudding was a once-a-week treat that we enjoyed throughout the year. It is fair to say that, after 10 years, the novelty wore off and it wasn't until recently, 30 years later, I rediscovered the delights of rice pudding and started playing with chocolate variations, eventually resulting in this recipe. When we come back from a windswept walk on West Wittering Beach, this is about as good as winter comfort food gets.

My only word of caution is to complete the cooking part in one move and do not part-cook and then reheat. Whatever you do to the recipe during the reheat, you will end up with a stodgy lump that is useful for rendering walls, but little else!

1 litre milk
90g granulated sugar
210g short grain rice

220g dark chocolate, grated

In a pan over a medium heat, gradually bring the milk and sugar to the boil.

Add the rice and simmer for about 25 minutes until the rice is tender and the milk has all been absorbed. You may need to add a little more milk during cooking to avoid the mixture drying out.

Add 190g of the chocolate and stir the mixture until melted.

Serve in bowls decorated with the remaining grated chocolate.

hot chocolate soup

prep 20 minutes ✶ serves 4

This is quick and easy but no less of a good recipe for that! We sampled a hot chocolate soup on a short trip to Belgium, and although on that occasion we found it too complex, this light soup is a real delight. By all means take this literally and eat it with a spoon, but we actually use this as a sauce to accompany the Chocolate Chip Brioche (see page 53) for a truly irresistible moment… or two. I am not entirely sure how it would work as a soup in the traditional sense but I suspect even the most hardened chocoholic would struggle.

1 litre milk
200g unsweetened cocoa
  powder

special equipment

food-processor

Pour the milk into a blender or food-processor and whizz for 15–20 minutes until you can't stand the noise any longer!

Boil the milk in a pan and gradually add the cocoa, whisking constantly. Reduce the heat to a very gentle simmer and continue whisking for 5 minutes until the chocolate is thick. To serve, pour it over the Chocolate Chip Brioche and really get stuck in.

chocolate fondue

prep 12 minutes (for simple method) or 20 minutes
(for advanced method) ✶ serves 6

If you want a party with all the swagger and swing of the 1970s, then nothing does it quite like a fondue, although car keys don't taste good even when covered in chocolate. You really don't need to splash out on a fondue set. These methods both work well – just keep the chocolate runny and stick to whatever you decide to dip. Remember, there are forfeits for dropping dippers off your fork into the chocolate!

ingredients (simple)

200g dark chocolate or milk
  chocolate (avoid white
  chocolate)
100ml double cream

to dip

fruits, biscuits, salted pretzels,
  mini doughnuts, marshmallows
  and anything else you fancy!

special equipment

bain-marie or heatproof bowl

Method (simple)

Melt the chocolate in a bain-marie or a heatproof bowl over a pan of water that boiled 5 minutes earlier and is now off the heat and cooling. Stir occasionally until smooth.

Add the cream and mix until smooth. Leave over the cooling bain-marie and get dipping!

ingredients (advanced)

75ml whipping cream
10g glucose syrup

10g maple syrup or honey
200g dark chocolate
100ml whole milk

Method (advanced)

Put the cream, glucose and maple syrup (or honey) in a pan and bring to the boil. Turn off the heat as soon as it boils.

Melt the chocolate in a bain-marie or a heatproof bowl over a pan of water that boiled 5 minutes earlier and is now off the heat and cooling. Stir occasionally until smooth.

Pour the cream mixture over the chocolate slowly and gradually, in small batches, stirring continually and vigorously with a flexible spatula. This helps combine the mixture and creates a creamy texture.

Leave over the cooling bain-marie and serve hot, or at room temperature, and dip away!

5

Savoury

The challenge with chocolate in savoury dishes is to make a comfortable association in the minds of guests; tricky when most entirely disassociate chocolate with their knife and fork. Most of these recipes are presented in a way that means you can leave disclosure of the secret ingredient until after everyone has tucked in, admired and complimented the wonderful, rich flavour. My favourite is the white chocolate pasta recipe, which is absolutely beautiful and always a surprising delight.

barcelona toast

There are no prizes for guessing where this was first tasted, and yes it was at breakfast, and yes it made me feel really good – or maybe that was the double espresso that went with it. Sometimes a little bit of what we fancy is just what we need.

1 baguette
100g dark chocolate

drizzle of extra virgin olive oil
flakes of coarse sea salt

Cut the baguette on a diagonal so that the medium–thick slices are elongated.

Pop the baguette slices under the grill until lightly golden on both sides – this does mean turning them over! Remove the bread but leave the grill on a low heat.

Coarsely grate the chocolate over the still warm bread so it is covered completely. Pop it back under the grill for about 1 minute, but on a low heat, and ensure the chocolate doesn't burn.

Remove and drizzle olive oil over the chocolate before sprinkling with a few salt flakes. This is not healthy, but tastes really great!

TIP
It may be psychological, but use a baguette – don't be tempted by other somewhat inferior alternatives!

chocolate fritters

prep 3 ½ hours including chilling ✶ makes 12

This is one of the more difficult recipes in the book, and one that has taken many attempts to evolve into a workable method. Having said that, I hope you will give it a go and feel that the time we have invested was well spent when it comes to the tasting. We still aren't sure whether these are sweet or savoury!

for the chocolate and mascarpone filling

110g dark chocolate
90g mascarpone cheese

for the semolina

320ml milk
¼ teaspoon vanilla extract
25g semolina
25g caster sugar
50g ground almonds

for the coating

100g blanched almonds,
  coarsely chopped
100g breadcrumbs
2 eggs, beaten
vegetable oil, for frying
caster sugar

special equipment

bain-marie or heatproof bowl
cooking tongs
deep-fat fryer

To make the chocolate and mascarpone filling, melt the chocolate in a bain-marie or a heatproof bowl over a pan of water that boiled 5 minutes earlier and is now off the heat and cooling. Stir occasionally until smooth. When melted, cool the chocolate for 5 minutes and then blend in the cheese. Chill the mixture for about 30 minutes so it is firm enough to handle, and then roll into 12 balls. Place the balls on a baking tray and chill for 1 hour.

To make the semolina, pour the milk and vanilla extract into a pan and bring to the boil. Remove from the heat. Add the semolina in a steady stream, stirring. Continue stirring while adding the sugar and bring the mixture to the boil. Turn down the heat and cook over a low heat for about 20 minutes, continuing to stir to stop it sticking. Pour the mixture into a shallow dish and leave to cool to room temperature.

Roll each chilled chocolate and mascarpone ball in the semolina before rolling the balls in the ground almonds.

To make the coating, combine the blanched almonds with the breadcrumbs. Dip the balls into the beaten eggs and roll them immediately in the breadcrumb mixture. Chill for 30 minutes.

Pour the vegetable oil into a deep-fat fryer and heat to 200°C. Using tongs, carefully deep-fry each ball for a few minutes until lightly golden. Do this in small batches before drying the balls on kitchen paper and rolling them in caster sugar.

chocolate calamares

prep 1 hour 30 minutes ✳ serves 2 as a main or 4 as a starter

Probably because the Spanish royal court had chocolate for 100 years before the rest of Europe, savoury recipes with chocolate are more refined and more accepted in Spain than in other parts of the world. That isn't to say we can't enjoy them as well, and this Catalan recipe is among the very best, especially when paired with a generous glass of a full-bodied Spanish red.

500g (finished weight) squid (see first step below)
4 tablespoons olive oil
2 garlic cloves
20g flaked almonds
1 large onion, finely chopped
½ teaspoon dried thyme
200ml white wine

4 large tomatoes, skinned and roughly chopped
10–20g dark chocolate
salt and freshly ground black pepper
tomato and onion salad or patatas bravas, to serve

Squid can be bought ready prepared, or you can prepare a whole squid from the fishmonger. If you are preparing the squid yourself, hold the sac and pull off the head and tentacles. Cut the tentacles into pieces. Remove the long bone from the sac and any jelly-like matter. Now rinse the sac under cold running water before cutting into rings.

Add half the oil to a pan and fry the garlic and almonds until lightly browned. Remove from the pan and set aside.

Soften the onion in the pan using the other half of the oil before adding the squid, bay leaf and thyme. Fry until the squid turns from translucent to opaque white before pouring in the wine.

Simmer the squid for 5 minutes in the pan and then add the tomatoes and season with salt and pepper. Cover, and simmer further until the squid is tender. This will take about 1 hour and can't be rushed.

In the meantime, take the almonds and garlic and make a paste using a pestle and mortar. Use some of the liquid from the pan to thin the paste a little.

Stir the paste into the simmering squid and add the chocolate. Leave the mixture to thicken before serving with a tomato and onion salad or patatas bravas.

spiced bbq ribs

prep 1 hour, plus overnight marinating ∗ serves 4–8

'Wow, what was on those?' This was my reaction to an otherwise entirely uneventful housewarming BBQ that friends of ours held two years ago. Admittedly, these friends enjoy experimenting with chocolate in savoury dishes and had played with the original recipe. Things hotted up further, however, when their new Mexican oven caught fire and burnt a hole in their decking.

60g unsweetened cocoa powder
60g light brown sugar
3 tablespoons chilli powder
2 tablespoons salt
½ clove garlic, finely chopped

1 tablespoon mustard powder
2 teaspoons ground ginger
1 teaspoon allspice
2 racks pork back ribs
baked potatoes and green salad, to serve

Make the spice mix by taking a large bowl and combining all the dry ingredients.

Take the pork ribs and rub the spice mix generously into the ribs. Wrap them tightly in clingfilm and leave them overnight in the fridge.

Before cooking, remove the ribs from the fridge and wait until they reach room temperature. Preheat the oven to 190°C/gas mark 5.

When at room temperature, put the ribs in a roasting tin and roast for 35–45 minutes. When tender, place the ribs on a grill tray (or on the barbecue) and brown both sides for about 10 minutes each side.

Serve with baked potatoes and a green salad.

TIP
Don't blacken the ribs too much on the barbecue – and don't cook on flammable decking!

penne with chocolate, pistachios and roquefort

prep 40 minutes ∗ serves 4

Originally this was a pretty straightforward recipe with no chocolate twist. That was until we began experimenting with dark chocolate in savoury food. While the addition of chocolate doesn't always work, sometimes it turns something good into something surprisingly great, especially in this example, where the chocolate contrasts beautifully with the salty Roquefort. We generally find it best to tell guests about the secret 'white' ingredient after they begin eating!

2 tablespoons olive oil
1 small onion, finely chopped
350g penne pasta
900ml dry white wine
2 tablespoons milk
1 teaspoon sea salt
75g shelled pistachios, coarsely
  chopped
90g dark chocolate, finely
  grated

for the sauce

90g white chocolate
125g mascarpone cheese
60g Roquefort cheese, finely
  grated
2 tablespoons whole milk

special equipment

bain-marie or heatproof bowl

Add the oil to a frying pan and sauté the onion over a medium heat until just transparent. Add the penne and stir well 2 minutes. Pour in the wine and milk and season to taste with the salt. Bring the whole lot to a boil, and then simmer until the pasta is cooked al dente.

For the sauce, melt the white chocolate in a bain-marie or a heatproof bowl over a pan of water that boiled 5 minutes earlier and is now off the heat and cooling. You have to be especially careful not to burn white chocolate and this process will help to avoid this. Stir occasionally until smooth. Remove the chocolate from the heat and stir in the mascarpone, Roquefort and milk.

Drain the penne and place in a heated serving bowl.

Pour the chocolate sauce over the top of the penne and sprinkle with the chopped pistachios before gently integrating everything. Serve the dish hot with the grated dark chocolate on top.

variation

If you find Roquefort cheese too strong, goat's cheese makes a great alternative.

lecco ravioli

prep 2½ hours ✳ serves 4

This is a somewhat complicated recipe that was devised and refined after sampling something similar in a restaurant in Lecco, Italy. Lecco happens to be home to one of Italy's most prestigious chocolate makers, so the recipe wasn't just a happy coincidence!

400g plain flour, plus extra
  for dusting
2 large eggs
2 tablespoons butter, melted

for the filling

1 tablespoon butter
250g cooked spinach, finely
  chopped
2 tablespoons grated dark
  chocolate

45g raisins
30g stale rye breadcrumbs
1 large egg, lightly beaten
1 tablespoon finely chopped
  fresh parsley
1 teaspoon plus 1 pinch sugar
90g butter, melted
90g ricotta cheese, grated
salt and freshly ground black
  pepper

Sift the flour and a pinch of salt on to a clean surface and make a well in the centre. Break the eggs into the well and mix them in with the butter. Add about 1 tablespoon of water, if necessary, to make a smooth dough.

Knead the dough on a lightly floured board until smooth and beginning to become elastic. Gather the dough up into a ball, wrap it in clingfilm and leave it to rest for 30–60 minutes at room temperature.

Melt the butter in a heavy-based frying pan over a medium heat and sauté the spinach for a minute or so before transferring it to a clean, cool bowl.

Add the chocolate, raisins, breadcrumbs, egg, parsley and sugar. Season to taste with salt and pepper. If the mixture is not firm, add more breadcrumbs.

'Wake up' the dough by rolling it out very thinly on a lightly floured surface. Cut out 8cm round pieces of dough and gently place two teaspoons of the filling into the centre. Fold each piece of dough in half and seal by pinching the edges and then pressing with a fork (for homemade authenticity!).

Using a slotted spoon, and handling the ravioli gently, cook the pasta in small batches in a large pot of salted, boiling water for 3–4 minutes. Transfer the ravioli to a serving bowl using a slotted spoon and stir through the melted butter and the ricotta before serving.

spanish fish

prep 1 hour 15 minutes ✶ serves 4

This savoury recipe combines chocolate and fish and originates from southern Spain where it is very popular. The dish may sound unusual but it is always appreciated and looks very convincing. The dish tastes fabulous and I have served it up many times to some extremely sceptical guests. In fact the more sceptical, the better the eventual outcome appears to be!

115g unsalted butter
350g onions, roughly chopped
1 tablespoon plain flour
250ml fruity white wine
30g dark chocolate, grated
(eat the remainder of the bar during cooking!)
12 button mushrooms, halved

450g fresh white fish, chopped into bite-size pieces
(I generally prefer cod, although do ensure you buy it from a sustainable source)
salt and freshly ground black pepper
sautéed potatoes and a simple onion and tomato salad, to serve

Melt the butter in a shallow pan and gently fry the onion until very soft and caramelised but largely uncoloured – this takes about 40 minutes.

Stir the flour into the pan, followed by the wine and 175ml water. Season with salt and pepper and add the chocolate.

Stir in the mushrooms and then add the fish. Cover and simmer for about 20 minutes, until fully cooked. Remove the fish and keep it warm.

Stir the sauce and add extra wine if necessary. Serve the sauce over the fish accompanied by sautéed potatoes and a simple onion and tomato salad.

spiced lamb stew

prep 30 minutes, plus 1–1½ hours cooking ∗ serves 6–8

This savoury dish probably has more chocolate than any other in this chapter, but it doesn't turn a lovely stew into a chocolate mush. It really does work and I would challenge you to try this on any meat-eaters with a weakness for a warming stew. If you are nervous, you can halve the chocolate on your first attempt, but I would suggest being courageous and going for it!

1kg lamb (use a cut such as leg that works well with stews), cut into chunks
50ml olive oil, plus 4 tablespoons to brown lamb
1 medium onion, finely chopped
1 large carrot, finely chopped
1 celery stick, finely chopped
2 garlic cloves, finely chopped
2 bay leaves
250ml red wine
60ml white wine vinegar

300ml lamb stock
90g dark chocolate
4 tablespoons walnuts, coarsely chopped
2 tablespoons raisins
3 tablespoons pine nuts
salt and freshly ground black pepper

special equipment

bain-marie or heatproof bowl

Heat the 4 tablespoons oil in a pan over a high heat and brown the lamb in batches. Remove from the pan and set aside.

Now heat the 50ml oil in a large casserole over a low heat. Add the onion, carrot, celery and garlic. Fry until the vegetables are soft but not brown – about 10–15 minutes. Add the meat and bay leaves and season with salt and pepper. Pour in the wine and cook on a medium heat until it evaporates and thickens – about 5 minutes.

Next add the vinegar and cook until it has entirely evaporated. Now you need to simmer the meat by adding the stock, covering and leaving on a low heat for about 1 hour. If the mixture begins to dry out, you are permitted to add more stock!

Melt the chocolate in a bain-marie or a heatproof bowl over a pan of water that boiled 5 minutes earlier and is now off the heat and cooling. Stir until smooth. Add the walnuts, raisins and pine nuts to the chocolate. Mix well.

Now add the chocolate mixture to the casserole, mixing well. Simmer gently for a further 15 minutes. Serve with a pile of rice and a green salad.

variations

None – don't touch change a thing!

fillet of beef with cocoa sauce

prep 30 minutes the day before, plus 24 hours chilling, plus 40 minutes on the day ∗ serves 4

This is without a shadow of a doubt my favourite savoury recipe using chocolate. Because Helen is a vegetarian, I can use this dish to gang up with the other girls in the house and enjoy the occasional morsel of succulent red meat. Much depends on the quality of the fillet, but it is assured to deliver succulence and surprise in equal measure.

The meat element is simply prepared and always delivers on taste. We have served it with asparagus tips, crusty bread or even creamy mash – then there are those good-old, hand-cut chunky chips, which are very hard to beat. Although the cocoa comes right at the end, it is fundamental to the recipe, and not just there for the shock factor!

750ml red wine
25ml Cognac
1 carrot, cut into small sticks
1 large onion, finely sliced
4 beef fillets
90g giant sultanas

40g butter
1 tablespoon unsweetened
  cocoa powder
salt and freshly ground pepper
sautéed potatoes and
  asparagus tips, to serve

To make the marinade, start the day before. Pour the wine and half the Cognac into a large dish. Add the carrot, onion, a pinch of salt and a twist of ground pepper.

Add the beef fillets and cover the dish with clingfilm. Refrigerate for 24 hours.

The following day, pour the remaining Cognac into a bowl and add the sultanas. Leave the sultanas to soak for 1 hour.

To make the cocoa sauce, take the marinade out of the fridge and lift out the beef fillets. Remove all the carrot and onion pieces and drain them well, using kitchen roll to dry them.

In a heavy frying pan, heat half the butter and cook the carrots and onions until they are caramelised. Pour in the remaining marinade juices and simmer on a low heat for 20 minutes.

After 20 minutes, strain the marinade and discard the vegetables, then rapidly boil it to reduce to a sauce. Remove from the heat and blend in the cocoa until you get a smooth, thick sauce. Add the raisins.

When ready to serve, heat the remaining butter over a medium–high heat and sear the beef fillets for a minute or two each side (if wanted rare). Place a fillet on each plate and drizzle the cocoa sauce all around (be generous with the sauce). Serve with sautéed potatoes and asparagus tips.

chicken mole

prep 1 ½ hours, plus 40 minutes baking ✷ serves 4

Without wishing to be overly controversial, I am not a fan of Mexican food. This dish, however, is an exception, although the recipe has come a long way from the version I was first given on a cocoa plantation trip to Venezuela. To be honest, the original has long gone, but from memory it had about six ingredients and consisted of basic chicken with some thick chocolate sauce. I hope you find this considerably more refined.

1.3kg chicken pieces (on the bone)
2 onions, roughly chopped
4 tablespoons almonds, blanched
2 tablespoons raisins
3 black peppercorns
2 teaspoons red chilli paste
2 garlic cloves, finely chopped
3 large tomatoes, skinned, peeled or chopped
50g breadcrumbs
1 tablespoon sunflower oil
25g dark chocolate, broken into pieces
salt and freshly ground black pepper
rice and green vegetables, to serve

special equipment

food-processor or blender

Arrange the chicken in the base of a large pan with half the onion, and then cover everything with cold water and simmer for 1 hour.

Remove the chicken and onion with a slotted spoon and keep the stock. Remove the skin from the chicken and cut the chicken into bite-size chunks. Put the pieces into an ovenproof dish.

Preheat the oven to 180°C/gas mark 4. Sauté the almonds in a dry frying pan until browned. Use a blender or food-processor to chop them finely, along with the raisins and peppercorns.

Add the chilli paste, 180ml water, the remainder of the onion, garlic, tomatoes and breadcrumbs to the blender and whizz until smooth.

Put the oil in a pan and sauté the smooth mixture over a medium heat for about 5 minutes.

Pour 1 cup of the reserved stock into a small pan and add the chocolate, stirring until it has melted. Be careful not to burn the chocolate. Add the sautéed mixture to the chocolate mix and season with salt and pepper. Pour the sauce over the chicken in the ovenproof dish and cover with a lid.

Cook in the oven for another 40 minutes. Serve hot with rice and green vegetables.

6

Drinks

We all know and love a classic homemade chocolate shake, but have you ever tried jazzing up a boozy tipple with chocolate or getting creative with your hot choc flavours? From the slightly obvious to the entirely odd, these nine cocoa-rich drinks will mean that even plain old tea will never seem quite the same again. Once you have started this journey, there is no turning back.

real hot chocolate

prep 10 minutes ∗ serves 4

Unbelievably, there is often ferocious debate about the content of drinking chocolate. For me, it has to be made of chocolate and not simply cocoa powder and sugar, which is a feeble imitation of what the drink should be. This method is simply devised to ensure the chocolate melts correctly, doesn't burn and isn't left solid in the base of the mug.

80g (20g per mug) dark
  chocolate, chopped roughly
600ml (150ml per mug)
  whole milk or soya milk
whipped cream, to serve

special equipment

bain-marie or heatproof bowl
blender or food processor
  (optional)

Melt all the chocolate in a bain-marie or a heatproof bowl over a pan of water that boiled 5 minutes earlier and is now off the heat and cooling. Stir occasionally until smooth.

Meanwhile, boil the milk in another pan and simmer while the chocolate melts. Pour the milk over the chocolate and stir the mixture with a wooden spoon until the chocolate is entirely integrated. Either whisk the mixture manually or in a blender or food-processor if you want to add a bubbly, light feel to the drink.

Pour the chocolate drink into 4 mugs, top each one with whipped cream (if using) and enjoy.

TIP
Try sprinkling
cocoa or
cinnamon on
top of the
cream

real chocolate milkshake

prep 20 minutes ∗ serves 4

No book on chocolate would be complete without a milkshake. I have discovered, much to my surprise, that while most children love milkshakes, many adults claim to have grown out of them through the unfortunate process of getting older. I cannot imagine why anyone would grow out of milkshakes – it's rather like not enjoying doing wheelies on your bike (or maybe that's just me!).

600ml whole milk, very cold
80g chocolate, broken
  in pieces (I advise dark
  chocolate to keep the
  sweetness under control)
12 large scoops vanilla ice
  cream, preferably one using a
  natural vanilla

chocolate syrup from a
  squeezy bottle (optional)
30g milk chocolate, grated

special equipment

4 tall glasses (prepared in the
  freezer for 10 minutes only)

Take 100ml of the milk and heat it to a vigorous simmer before adding 40g of the chocolate. Allow the chocolate to melt before placing it in a cold bowl and putting in the freezer for 15 minutes to cool.

Put the remaining chocolate and cold milk with the ice cream in a food-processor and whizz for 1 minute. Add the cold milk-and-chocolate mix and whizz for another 30 seconds.

Take the glasses from the freezer and decorate the inside of each one with a swirl of chocolate syrup. Pour in the milkshake and decorate with the grated milk chocolate. Throw in a massive straw and drink the milkshake between wheelies!

spiced eskimo

prep 10 minutes ✳ serves 4

This is a simple and delightful chilled chocolate drink, effectively a posh milkshake. The addition of malt to the milk gives a very homely taste and feel, and the cinnamon adds warmth.

8 teaspoons malt powder
pinch of cinnamon
1 litre milk
8 scoops chocolate ice cream
500ml whipped cream
50g dark chocolate, grated

special equipment

4 tall glasses
blender or food-processor
  (optional)

Beat the malt powder, cinnamon and milk in a medium bowl until well combined. This can be done with a blender or food-processor, but be aware that the longer you do this, the more air and volume it will add to the milk.

Place 2 scoops of ice cream into each glass, and pour the milk over the ice cream.

Decorate with cream and grated chocolate on top. Use a straw to drink, and don't forget to blow bubbles!

variations

Adding an alcoholic shot or two turns this from a kid's delight into an adult winner. Drambuie works particularly well, as does any good-quality whisky such as Bowmore. We do from time to time add other spices, including the merest hint of nutmeg, which works nicely with the malt.

montezuma's revenge

prep 10 minutes ✳ serves 4

Let's start with the name 'Montezuma's Revenge'. Cocoa, in its unrefined form, was consumed by the Aztecs. Moctezuma II himself, the ruler of the Aztec civilisation, used it as an aphrodisiac. Unfortunately, in this raw, unrefined form, it actually has a laxative effect.

You would have assumed that a contradiction of that magnitude would have quickly become obvious, but that dichotomy is one origin of the phrase 'Montezuma's Revenge'. In reality, the origins are in the somewhat more depressing fact that Monty was stoned to death by his own people for introducing the invading conquistadores as the arrival of a long lost god (see page 7).

This little tipple may seem innocent in comparison, but it should bring a smile to your face!

80g (20g per mug) dark
  chocolate, chopped roughly
600ml (150ml per mug)
  whole milk or soya milk
3 tablespoons brandy
100ml espresso or very strong
  coffee

pinch of ground chilli
whipped cream (optional)

special equipment

bain-marie or heatproof bowl
food-processor or blender

Melt all the chocolate in a bain-marie or a heatproof bowl over a pan of water that boiled 5 minutes earlier and is now off the heat and cooling. Stir occasionally until smooth.

Meanwhile, boil the milk in another pan and simmer while the chocolate melts. Pour the milk over the chocolate and stir with a wooden spoon until entirely integrated.

Pour the mixture into a food-processor or blender and add the brandy, espresso and the pinch of chilli powder. Whizz for 1 minute before pouring the chocolate mixture into 4 large mugs and decorating each one with whipped cream, if using.

mocha brazilia

prep 10 minutes serves 4

If you have spotted a few coffee and chocolate recipes creeping in, then you would be right to guess that I love both of them, because together they are irresistible. I have almost as many coffee machines as chocolate gadgets, but for this I have used the old stove-top espresso maker and some top-quality medium ground beans. It certainly delivers quite a big punch, which is probably best not taken directly before bed, unless you want to stay awake all night. I've given the quantities in mugs here to keep things simple. Just choose your favourite mugs and take it away.

3 mugs whole milk
20g granulated sugar
110g dark chocolate, finely
  chopped
1 mug fresh coffee (ensure it
  is fresh and strong, probably
  equivalent to a double
  espresso per mug)

whipped cream and grated
  chocolate, to decorate

special equipment

stove-top espresso maker
blender or food-processor

Boil the milk and sugar together in a pan and simmer for about 1 minute. Take the pan off the heat and stir in the chocolate and the freshly made coffee. Keep back about 20g of the chocolate for decoration.

Blend the mixture with a blender or food-processor for about 2 minutes so it becomes light and slightly airy. Pour the drink into the mugs and top with whipped cream and grated chocolate.

malaysian chocolate tea

prep 10 minutes ✳ serves 4

If you have not yet sampled Malaysian Teh Tarik (as I hadn't until recently), made with hot milk and tea, then you have missed out on a brilliantly light, bubbly, sweet drink. This is my attempt at improving the recipe by getting some chocolate into the mix to add richness. It works so well that normal tea will seem decidedly pale and pasty afterwards!

120g dark chocolate, broken into pieces
20g fine black tea
65ml sweetened condensed milk
unsweetened cocoa powder, for sprinkling

special equipment

bain-marie or heatproof bowl
blender or food-processor (optional)

Melt the chocolate in a bain-marie or a heatproof bowl over a pan of water that boiled 5 minutes earlier and is now off the heat and cooling. Stir occasionally until smooth.

Pour 500ml boiling water over the tea. Leave for 5 minutes to brew and then strain through a fine sieve. Discard the tea leaves

Slowly pour a third of the freshly brewed tea over the melted chocolate, whisking all the time. Now pour in the remainder of the tea, whisking constantly.

When smooth, add the condensed milk. Normally you would pour the tea from one glass to another to introduce some air, but because the mixture is so thick this is best done with a blender or food-processor. Whizz until nice and foamy before serving, sprinkled with cocoa powder.

brandy alexander

prep 10 minutes ✶ makes 4 cocktails

In my copy of the long out-of-print *American Barman*, published in 1951, it says that this drink is named after the Russian Tsar Alexander II, but in fact I have read many other accounts of the naming of this variation on the gin-based Alexander cocktail. In any event, no self-respecting chocolate book is complete without a recipe for one of the best cocktails to kick off an evening soirée.

a handful of ice cubes
120ml brandy
120ml Crème de Cacao
120ml double cream (always
  use equal measures of
  brandy, Crème de Cacao and
  double cream – just scale the
  quantity up or down)
fresh nutmeg, for grating

special equipment

cocktail shaker, cocktail
  glasses and strong arms!

Put the ice cubes, brandy, Crème de Cacao and cream in a cocktail shaker.

Shake well, and strain into four cocktail glasses.

Grate nutmeg over the top of each and enjoy.

variations

Adapt this into the celebrated Pavlova, which uses equal quantities of vodka, Crème de Cacao and cream.

cheeky chimp

prep 10 minutes ✱ serves 4

For many years one of our most popular chocolate truffles was a fresh banana and cream ganache wrapped in a perfectly thick milk chocolate shell. They were irresistibly moreish and this prompted us to experiment further and create a long and boozy drink to enjoy on lazy summer evenings. Definitely a grown-up milkshake, but that is no bad thing.

50ml banana liqueur, chilled
30ml Crème de Cacao
60ml chocolate syrup, plus 10ml for decoration
3 scoops chocolate ice cream plus 250ml whole milk, or 350ml chocolate milk, chilled

60ml whipped cream, to decorate
40g milk chocolate, grated, to decorate

special equipment

blender or food-processor or a large cocktail shaker
tall glasses

Use a blender or food-processor (or large cocktail shaker if you are feeling brave and strong) to whizz the ingredients for a few seconds until smooth.

Pour the cocktail into tall glasses and finish with whipped cream, a drizzle of chocolate syrup and grated chocolate.

One glass is probably enough!

montezuma's martini

prep 10 minutes ✳ serves 4-8

What happens when you put ten bartenders in a room and ask them to make a Martini? Ten different drinks come back at you: choose from gin or vodka, vermouth or not, stir it or shake it, float an olive or sink some lemon garnish. One drink, so many options. Here is one more you may not have tried – this will add a touch of controversy to the Martini debate. This serves 4 generously – or could make up to 8 smaller cocktails.

chocolate syrup, for swirling
120ml chocolate milk, cold
150ml vanilla vodka, from the
  freezer
120ml Crème de Cacao
120ml Irish Cream liqueur

40g dark chocolate shavings,
  to decorate

special equipment

large cocktail shaker
Martini glasses, placed in the
freezer 10 minutes before

When you're ready to make the cocktails, take the Martini glasses directly from the freezer and swirl a little chocolate syrup around the inside for decoration.

Half-fill a cocktail shaker with ice and pour in the chocolate milk, vanilla vodka, Crème do Cacao and Irish Cream liqueur. Shake.

Strain the mixture into the Martini glasses. Decorate each glass with shaved chocolate before serving.

Shaken
not stirred!

index

resources

a note on ingredients and equipment

We have tried to stick to using ingredients and equipment that is widely available from any good shop. Even the Easter egg doesn't require industrial investment in moulds and spinning equipment! Mostly the ingredients should be available from local food stores.

Montezuma's

To find out more about Montezuma's, visit www. montezumas.co.uk, or follow us on Twitter (@montezumas) or Facebook (Montezuma's Chocolates).

mole, chicken 149
Montezuma
    (Motecuhzoma) II,
    Emperor 7, 157
Montezuma's 8–9
Montezuma's Martini 164
Montezuma's revenge 7, 157
mousses: crunchy olive oil
    and chocolate mousse 88
sunshine 86
mushrooms: Spanish fish
    142

N
nibs 10
nutcase: chestnut and
    chocolate terrine 83
nuts: clusters 20
    marbled three-nut 'get-
    going' bars 60–1
    nut and chocolate strudel
    68
    see also almonds, pecans
    etc

O
oats: chocolate fruit crumble
    121
    marbled three-nut 'get-
    going' bars 60–1
olive oil and chocolate
    mousse 88
onions: chicken mole 149
    Spanish fish 142
oranges: chocolate brioche
    with orange and ginger
    123–5
    chocolate citrus tart 73
    Dolomite chocolate affair
    82
    orange and cardamom
    blancmange 81
    orange and geranium
    chocolate soufflé 111
    orangettes 21
    ricotta, chocolate and
    orange turnovers 122
    sunshine 86
    zesty orange squares 30–1

P
panforte 50
pasta: lecco ravioli 141

penne with chocolate,
    pistachios and
    Roquefort 138
pastries: chocolate and
    pistachio filo parcels 69
    nut and chocolate strudel
    68
    pithivier 74–5
    ricotta, chocolate and
    orange turnovers 122
    see also tarts
peanuts: marbled three-nut
    'get-going' bars 60–1
pears belle Hélène 117
pecan nuts: marbled three-
    nut 'get-going' bars 60–1
    salted pecan and chocolate
    pie 67
penne with chocolate,
    pistachios and
    Roquefort 138
peppermint: chocolate and
    mint zabaione 95
    chocolate mintmocha
    whirls 91
    cocoa mint soft jelly 92
    peppermint creams 33
pine nuts: spiced lamb stew
    145
pistachios: chocolate and
    pistachio filo parcels 69
    nut and chocolate strudel
    68
    penne with chocolate,
    pistachios and
    Roquefort 138
pithivier 74–5
plums: chocolate and plum
    bakes 70–1
pork: spiced BBQ ribs 137
potatoes: torta di patate 52
praline: chocolate hens' eggs
    37
    praline ice cream 100

R
raisins: chicken mole 149
    clusters 20
    Dolomite chocolate affair
    82
    fillet of beef with cocoa
    sauce 146
    lecco ravioli 141

ricotta, chocolate and
    orange turnovers 122
    spiced lamb stew 145
    white chocolate granola
    34
raspberries: white chocolate
    and summer fruit fools
    85
raspberry jam: chocolate
    trifle 78–9
ravioli, lecco 141
real chocolate milkshake
    153
real hot chocolate 152
rice: dark chocolate risotto
    126
rice cereal: clusters 20
    marbled three-nut 'get-
    going' bars 60–1
ricotta cheese: chocolate and
    orange turnovers 122
    lecco ravioli 141
risotto, dark chocolate 126
rocher, classic 18
Roquefort, penne with
    chocolate, pistachios and
    138
rose geranium oil see
    geranium oil
roulade, classic double
    chocolate 45
rum: chocolate hens' eggs 37

S
salted caramel puddings 115
salted pecan and chocolate
    pie 67
scones, chocolate 57
semolina: chocolate fritters
    135
sesame seeds: crunchy olive
    oil and chocolate mousse
    88
sherry: nutcase: chestnut and
    chocolate terrine 83
sorbets: chilli and lime
    chocolate sorbet 104
    three-minute delight:
    cocoa, mango and chilli
    sorbet 103
soufflés: Arctic soufflés 102
    orange and geranium
    chocolate soufflé 111

acknowledgements

We would like to thank the following people for
their help and support while researching, writing and
testing the recipes in this book:

Tara O'Sullivan, our editor, who really did have the
patience of a saint;

Steve Calver, for spending time many years ago teaching
us the basics of the art;

Stacey Bedford, our tolerant PA who tirelessly kept
us organised whilst researching and
scribbling notes everywhere;

Gill Hill, our head chocolatier, who had to taste more recipes than
should be humanly possible; and finally,

All those wonderful people who work in the chocolate industry
who strive to produce ethically sound, quality chocolate and
who really care about the
society they impact.